How to Be Wise and Successful

That It May Be Well
with You

Warren W. Burnham

This book is available at
amazon and Barnes + Noble

ISBN 978-1-68570-951-8 (paperback)
ISBN 978-1-68570-952-5 (digital)

Christian Faith Publishing
832 Park Avenue
Meadville, PA 16335
www.christianfaithpublishing.com

Printed in the United States of America

My First Bible

⌒⊙⌒

"**N**o. I don't want a Bible for Christmas! We have enough Bibles around here!"

Those were the words of my response to my mother when she asked, "Warren, do you want a Bible for Christmas?"

I was fourteen years old. That was a long time ago.

Well, I DID receive a Bible for Christmas that year! It was one of a very few gifts. My parents were not rich financially.

For some reason, I read that Bible, a King James Version with a black cover. My name was on the front. I read it a lot as a teenager. It influenced my life greatly then and has ever since.

> Thy Word is a lamp unto my feet, and a
> light unto my path. (Psalm 119:105 KJV)

The most important thing I can ever tell you is to make a habit of reading the Bible every day! Especially Proverbs!

You Decide: Faith in Christ

⁓⊙⊙⊙⊙

1951, age sixteen in a small country church, at night

There I sat, somewhat alone, on the back row of the church. No brother, no sister, no mother or father, nor friend beside me. Just me with my thoughts and feelings. Probably no more than fifty or sixty folks in the building.

The sermon was just over. The invitation hymn, "Just as I Am," was being sung.

There I was, listening and thinking and feeling, as a sixteen-year-old. I was taking it all in. All to myself.

For the first time in my life, *I realized that I needed Christ in my life.* For real. I needed and wanted to make a public decision. *A commitment to faith in Jesus Christ. And I did.*

The process that led to that very intense moment of decision was reading the Bible. I had begun reading the Bible at age fourteen. For me, it was simple but powerful and meaningful. You may want to consider daily Bible reading, especially Psalm 1 and Proverbs.

> So then faith cometh by hearing, and hear-
> ing by the Word of God. (Romans 10:17 KJV)

True and Personal—Psalm One

❧⊙❧

This happened to me during the 1970s. We were living in the suburbs of Baltimore, Maryland. I was attending a Christian life conference and was introduced to Psalm 1. Again. I sort of like rediscovered it. Memorized it.

Since then, I've repeated it to myself more times than I can even come close to remembering. It's a powerful psalm. Full of guidance, truth, and wisdom. I strongly encourage you to memorize it too!

It helps you to know how to "make it." What to do! What not to do! And what to think about! How to be successful!

> Blessed is the man that walketh not in the counsel of the ungodly, nor standeth in the way of sinners, nor sitteth in the seat of the scornful.
>
> But his *delight* is in the Law of the Lord; and in his law doth he *meditate* day and night.
>
> And he shall be like a tree planted by the *rivers of water*, that bringeth forth his fruit in his season; his leaf also *shall not wither*; and *whatsoever he doeth shall prosper.*
>
> The ungodly are not so: but are like the chaff which the wind driveth away. Therefore the ungodly shall not stand in the judgment, nor sinners in the congregation of the righteous. For the LORD knoweth the way of the righteous: but the way of the ungodly shall perish. (Psalm 1:4–6 KJV)

Believe in Angels

There we were as young teenagers, my brother Larry and myself, swimming in the Ocmulgee River, about a mile from our home in Abbeville, Georgia.

Downstream and upstream. We did both although it had a very strong current!

There was a tree on the bank where we often calmly entered the water like otters. Other times, we would climb high up into the tree and jump! Not being able to see what might be floating beneath the surface of the reddish water, we never gave any thought of alligators or snakes or the swiftness of the water. We would just jump, spending hours totally alone. Unsupervised!

In retrospect, years later, *I believe angels must have been there looking after us.* I've gone back as an adult to visit the place. I was shocked at the thought of our swimming on many hot summer days there.

For He shall give His angels charge over you
to keep you in all your ways. (Psalm 91:11 KJV)

Believe that Maybe an Angel Helped You

cAOCAs

It was 1942, as I recall, when my brother Larry fell out of the tree landing on his back in a pile of pecan leaves. The piles of leaves were smoking on fire beneath the surface, but not blazing.

Larry was a six-year-old kid that obviously liked to climb trees, take some risks, and not being too careful when he slipped and fell.

Mom and Dad and I were on the ground raking the leaves into a pile in our backyard. Not looking up, we were somewhat unaware of Larry being in the tree. When suddenly, there he was flat on his back and on the pile of leaves.

Unconscious for a few moments! But not really hurt! Thankful for the pile of leaves. *Just in the right place at the right time.* They were smoldering, but he was not even scorched.

Reading the Bible daily helps to remind us that *we possibly and likely have angels about us, protecting us in ways we don't even recognize* or acknowledge at the time.

> For He shall give his angels charge over thee
> to keep thee in all thy ways. (Psalm 91:11 KJV)

Be Thankful for Your Freedom

❧❧❧

I was in school, first grade, six years old, in Abbeville, Georgia, in December 1941. We were informed that Japan had bombed Pearl Harbor, waging war on the United States.

All it was to me was information. No pain. No tears. There I was safe as could be in a nice, quiet, cozy classroom with about twenty-five of my peers.

Unaware of the devastation. The deaths. The drownings. The fires. The shock. Nature of the tragedy. Innocent people. Thousands killed.

Abbeville was a quiet, small, rural-like town in South Georgia, the county seat of Wilcox County. One post office and one red light. Two pharmacies. Seven grocery stores. Two banks. A couple of gas stations. One sawmill. Several small farms outside of town. Also, one theater and two churches. Peaceful. Calm. Place where the country farmers came to town only on Saturday afternoon to buy groceries.

So, between 1941 and 1945, during World War II, I lived like so many others in a safe nest, somewhat totally undisturbed.

Reading the Bible daily helps to make us aware that safety and freedom are tremendous blessings. *Reading the Bible teaches gratitude.*

> Know ye that the Lord He is God; it is He that hath made us, and not we ourselves; we are his people and the sheep of his pasture.
>
> Enter into His gates with thanksgiving, and into His be thankful unto Him and bless His Name.
>
> For the Lord is good; His mercy is everlasting; and His truth endureth to all generations. (Psalm 100:3–5 KJV)

Be Alert Every Day

⁓◌◔◌⁓

We were preteens. Larry, my younger brother, and myself. Just the two of us were wading in the water of a flowing spring between Abbeville and Fitzgerald, Georgia. The water was clear as a colorless glass. It was a beautiful sunny day. Warm summertime. Why were we there all alone, I don't know. Not really a wise thing to be in water alone, *not able to swim yet and unaware of the depth of the water.*

So it happened! Larry stepped into a hole deeper than expected. Water was over his head. It just happened that I was nearby standing in more shallow water. Quickly I was able to reach him. I caught him by the arm and pulled him out of the deeper water to safety. It all happened in seconds. Nothing was ever said about it. No one other than the two of us ever knew about it. But what would have happened if I had not been there and able to reach him? Within a second. A moment.

Not all moments in life are the same. Some moments we make decisions or do things or say things that might greatly influence our lives or the life of someone else. *We may need to pray that God keeps us alert, wise, and available at all times for our own well-being and others.*

> And that, knowing the time that now it is
> high time to awake out of sleep: for now is our
> salvation nearer than when we believed. (Romans
> 13:11 KJV)

Be Thankful for Your
Pug Nose Mountains

⚜

My wife did not believe there was such a place in my childhood life named "Pug Nose Mountain." So I said to her, "If you don't believe me, call my sister," who is also in her senior years. She did.

My sister responded immediately, "Yes, there is/was a place called Pug Nose Mountain."

Admittedly, it is not part of the Rocky Mountains in the West. Not a part of the Appalachian Mountains in the East. Not a Mount Sinai or Mount Horeb in the Middle East.

But it was and is a real place named in our childhood. It was near our home where I grew up in South Georgia.

It was a hill, a steep hill that we slid down, covered with grassy slopes. It was a great place to slide down using large flattened pieces of cardboard.

The four of us siblings spent hours together sliding down those grassy slopes. A fun place! Kaye, my youngest sister, says we named Pug Nose Mountain after her.

Today, years later, in our adulthood, Pug Nose Mountain is a wonderful childhood memory. Just us. Brothers and sisters!

Reading the Bible daily helps us to remember some of the wonderful experiences of our youth.

> *Remember now thy Creator in the days of thy youth*, while the evil days come not nor the years draw nigh, when thou shalt say, I have no pleasure in them. (Ecclesiastes 12:1 KJV)

Realize the True Meaning
of Rich or Poor

಄ᎨᎨᏂ

It was a very cold, windy, early evening in January or February, already dark. There, my mother and I were cutting wood with a crosscut saw. Some of you may not know what a crosscut saw is. It demands manual labor by two people. One person on each end of the saw. I was about ten or twelve years old. I'm not sure where my dad was at the time, but Mom and I were cutting up wood for our woodburning stove, which was used to keep our house warm. We had no central heat or cooling system.

In fact, I was greatly blessed! We had no TV. No cell phones. No computers. No refrigerator. Just an icebox. No family car until my brother, Larry, and I bought one with our paper route money.

Born in 1935, during the Great Depression era, *I was blessed to grow up poor compared to today's standards.*

What I was blessed with was a strong work ethic. Discipline, respect for authority, church attendance every Sunday, and Bible reading in the home. Rich with the principles and values that matter! Poor in things that really don't matter!

Reading the Bible daily helps a person, a family, and a society know the true definitions of the words rich *and* poor.

> For riches are not forever: and doth the crown endure to every generation? (Proverbs 27:24 KJV)

Remember Small Deeds
May Not Be Small

⸙⸕⸙

The school year was 1952–1953. I was a senior in Abbeville High School. It was one of four high schools in Wilcox County. Others were Pitts, Pineview, and Rochelle. One major decision facing me was which of two classes I would take for my final year. I had a choice of taking another, in fact, a fourth, agriculture class or taking French. In French, I would be the only boy in an all-girls class. I decided, admittedly with a small bit of reluctance, to take the French.

I knew that I didn't want to be a farmer. For sure. All I knew about farming was learned the three summers I spent on my grandfather Burnham's farm when I was ages eight, nine, and ten.

However, the one thought that I have remembered, all these years, from the three years of agriculture classes was the motto written on the table in front of the classroom where the teacher sat. *"Small deeds done are greater than large deeds planned."*

While I remember little or no French, I do remember that motto. A worthy thought to remember! So giving someone *a smile*, a "How are you?" *eye contact*, *a phone call*, or a *tip* to your garbage collector may be a lot more important than you think!

Think about it and remember to read a chapter in Proverbs today and Psalm 1.

Jesus said:

> Whosoever shall give drink unto one of these little ones a cup of cold water only in the name of a disciple, verily I say unto you, he shall in no wise lose his reward. (Matthew 10:42 KJV)

Learn to Live with Your Past and Childhood

⤳⤳⤳

I t was many years ago, during World War II, 1943, before my fourteenth birthday that I started reading the Bible regularly.

My brother, Larry, and I in broad daylight stole some discarded old scrap iron. It wasn't locked up or anything like that. It was just piled up in plain view on the ground outside a building, seemingly worthless. Where it came from or what they were going to do with the scrap iron, we had no idea. So we just casually gathered it up, put it in our little red wagon, and hauled it off to be sold for the war cause. We, of course, kept the money. At that time, its worth was less than $2.00 or $3.00. But it wasn't ours to be sold! We were thieves! Our parents never learned of our behavior.

The amount of scrap iron we took was so small that it likely was never missed from the pile of scrap.

I'm not even sure that we rationalized the behavior to ease our conscience. It just didn't bother us with any guilt. We were kids just busy helping the war effort and ourselves.

So what do you do with situations and events or behavior that happened years ago? We cannot, for sure, rewrite our history. Oftentimes, there is nothing we can do about our past!

The issue may be very small or great, but you can't do anything about it. You can't change it!

That is why reading the Bible daily is so important to discover verses of truth, like the following:

> If we confess our sin, He is faithful and just to forgive us our sin and cleanse us from all unrighteousness. (1 John 1:9 KJV)

Maybe Enjoy a Pig for a Pet

"Jo-cee" was the name of our pet pig. There were five of us siblings, two girls and three boys. Jo-cee belonged to all five of us children growing up in the small town of Abbeville, Georgia.

My dad bought Jo-cee for a nickel from my grandfather Burnham. Jo-cee was the runt of the litter. She was a very small, petite, ugly little four-legged animal. I don't have any idea how much he weighed when dad brought him home.

We did not live on a farm; we just had a yard in a small town. So at first, for months, Jo-cee slept and lived in a box on our back porch.

Seriously, I'm not kidding. Finally, he went to the yard and grew to be a two hundred-pound hog. Still our pet! *We would scratch him on his stomach. He would roll over like a dog to be petted.*

Thus, living in town, not enough yard to keep him, we had to sell Jo-cee. We realized eventually that somebody would eat our pig. A sad ending to a great story. But it was a fun experience for all five children while we had him. We still enjoy remembering Jo-cee. *Life in general is often a bitter-sweet experience.* Wonderful and bad wrapped in one.

Reading the Bible daily *helps us to understand life* somewhat. Not entirely! And to accept it! And go on! Especially Psalm 1 and Proverbs.

> Remember now thy Creator in the days of thy youth, while the evil days came not, nor the years draw nigh, when then shall say, I have no pleasure in them. (Ecclesiastes 12:1 KJV)

Poor Might Be Better
than Pampered

⚜

Rastus and Rex were our family dogs in South Georgia in the 1950s and 1960s. Rastus was a black, short-haired stray dog we found when he was only a puppy. Not pretty even as a puppy. Just a mutt. Homeless. Finding him, all alone, my brother and I carried him home with us. He had no collar. No identification. He grew to be a large, tall-standing dog. Handsome and proud!

Then there was Rex. He was white and longhaired. He came to us, I recall, fully grown. How, I don't remember. He was about half the height of Rastus, a pretty dog.

They were buddies. Different color. Different in size and length of hair. They both lived together under our house. Never came into the house. They were yard dogs! Neither one was ever carried to a veterinarian. We never bought dog food for them. They ate only scraps from our table. Leftover people food. Even chicken bones!

We loved those dogs. They were definitely family pets but never overly pampered. Both lived to be in their upper teens. Died a natural death after I left home.

The truth of the matter, I myself personally grew up poor compared to today's standards. No TV. No central heating or air. No car in the family for years. We walked everywhere. Sparse furniture in the house. I wore holes in my pants before it was popular. Saved my own money to buy my first bicycle.

I'm thankful that I grew up somewhat like Rastus and Rex. Not overly pampered. Just glad to be in the house! Poor is often better than pampered!

Reading the Bible daily gives you wisdom and a sense of gratitude for daily bread and a roof over your head.

> Better is the poor that walketh in his integrity than he that is perverse in his lips and is a fool. (Proverbs 19:1 KJV)

Wake Up to Your World

$\sim\!\!\infty\!\!\sim$

It was the splash of cold well water in my face that woke me up every summer morning, June, July, and August of 1945. I was only ten years old. World War II was just over. I was spending the "out of school" days working in the fields on my grandfather's farm.

Every day, my first event was drawing water in a bucket from the well. There was no hot water. No running water. Nevertheless, about daybreak, I would gather water into my cupped hands and splash it into my face. Cold. Shock. Suddenly and immediately awaken! Eyes wide awake. Alert. Ready to face the day.

While I was wide awake to the day, my day on the farm, I had no awareness of the rest of the world. What was going on? What had been happening in a world at war. The destruction. The deaths. The sorrows. The tears.

Reading the Bible daily helps us to be mentally and spiritually awake and aware to face our very troubled world.

> And that, knowing the time, that it is high time to awake out of sleep: for now is our salvation nearer than when we believed. (Romans 13:11 KJV)

The Earlier You Learn the Better

☙

Two mules and a four-wheeled farm wagon were our transportation to town every Saturday afternoon. The wagon was the same kind that you see in the old western movies of yesteryears.

Yes, many rural folk, countryfolk, in Georgia, like my grandparents, were still using those wagons in the 1940s. So we rode in the wagon, pulled by two mules, not horses, every Saturday afternoon from granddad's farm to Rhine, Georgia. A distance of a few miles.

We had worked all week, Monday through Friday, in the hot summer sun in the fields. Sweating. Long hours. Sunup to sundown. Hoeing weeds from peanuts, corns, and cotton. Manual labor!

So! Going to town on Saturday afternoon was a *big deal!* To be rewarded with a Pepsi-Cola and a bar of candy. Something we anticipated all week. Pepsi was a nickel! A bar of candy was a nickel in 1945. I was a ten-year-old kid.

Reading the Bible daily and hard work, early in life, helps to teach us *gratitude for simple things, small blessings!*

> In everything give thanks; for this is the will of God in Christ Jesus concerning you. (1 Thessalonians 5:18 KJV)

> Remember now thy Creator in the days of thy youth. (Ecclesiastes 12:1 KJV)

Learn to Receive as well as to Give

⊱⊶⊷⊰

This happened sometime during 1953, a few miles south of Rhine, Georgia. I was only eighteen years old and an assistant pastor of Sharon Baptist Church, preaching twice monthly. Dad was the senior pastor. Sharon was a country church. Very country! Lots of less than middle-class folk were members. Humble folk. Honest, good people.

Anyway, this was during an annual revival meeting. Practice was for the guest speaker, the pastor, and me to often visit the homes of various members for a meal.

This particular day, the three of us were seated at the dinner table of one of the members. The meal was served. Beside each plate were a fork, a knife, and a spoon. All the knives and forks were rusty. Yes. Only the spoons were clean, shiny, with no rust.

Without a word being said by any of the three of us, their guests, we just quietly used only our spoons. Eating as if it was a feast. Provided for us by simple, poor, but very loving people and very hospitable!

Point. There are times it's a good lesson to learn. Not only are we to give to people. *It's good to humbly receive from people who have less.* It's their best. They too want to give.

> And there came *a certain poor widow* and she threw in two mites which made a farthing... this poor widow hath cast more in than all they which have cast into the treasury... She *of her want did cast in all that she had.* (Mark 12:42–43 KJV)

Listen to Encouraging,
Hopeful Words

⟡⟡⟡⟡

FDR called them "Fireside Chats" in the 1940s, during World War II. That was before television. The chats from the president of the United States were heard on the radio. People listened attentively.

I recall those nights sitting around the fireplace at our grand-father Burnham's home near Rhine, out in the country. Those were the days in rural Georgia before electric lights. The only light was kerosene lamps and the fire in the fireplace. The burning wood was called a "lightered knot." The stump of a pine tree. The fire burned brightly and easily. And it was hot.

In that setting, we often gathered, the several of us, and listened to the radio. Glad to hear the news from the outside world and the president. Often his words would be instructive, encouraging, and hopeful.

In the darkest of nights and situations, positive and encouraging words can make a tremendous difference. Helpful! Uplifting! Hopeful!

> Thy words have upholden him that was falling, and thou hast strengthened the feeble knees. (Job 4:4 KJV)

> As cold water to a thirsty soul, so is good news from a far country. (Proverbs 25:25 KJV)

Look Up at the Stars

◈

1950–1953

I was a teenager. Early in the morning hours. Before dawn. Before the first twinkle of light. The moon was still very visible. All four years of high school, I was up and out. Wide awake. Delivering newspapers. *Atlanta Journal, Atlanta Constitution, Macon Telegraph*. Seven days a week, 365 days a year.

Rain or shine. Sleet or snow. Hot or cold. My brother and I were up before school hours, delivering newspaper door-to-door in Abbeville. A small town of about one thousand people in South Georgia.

One main thing that I recall from those early morning experiences was viewing the stars in the wintertime. Walking, I spent a lot of time looking up, viewing the stars. Aware of the darkness of the sky and the brightness of the stars.

I confess that while walking, looking up, wide awake, I would often pray, talking out loud.

Reading the Bible daily encourages us to look up and see the stars, even when the sky of your life may be at its darkest.

> I will lift up mine eyes unto the hills from whence cometh my help. My help cometh from the Lord, which made heaven and earth. (Psalm 121:1–2 KJV)

Watch Out for
Estranged Alligators

လတ္တြလ

It was an early, gloomy, rainy morning. The wee hours in fact. Still dark. Sun not up, but we were, my brother and I, walking, delivering newspapers door-to-door to homes in our small town of Abbeville, Georgia. Larry and I were still in our early teens. Delivering papers was our job every day before school.

Anyway, it was on one of those mornings that we almost stumbled over a three-foot alligator right in the middle of the street. How could a live alligator be there in the middle of the street? No river, stream, or pond anywhere nearby. Made no sense!

Nevertheless, we went on about our job. We left the alligator alone where he was. Never to see him again. Caring for estranged alligators was not our expertise!

In life, it's not uncommon to wonder how or why something happens. It may cause us to stumble. We have questions with no clear answers. Our best and the only honest answer is, "I don't know."

Reading the Bible daily, especially Psalm 1 and Proverbs, helps us with "I don't know" answers to the estranged alligators that may almost cause us to stumble in life.

> For now we see through a glass darkly; but then face to face; now I know in part; but then shall I know even as also I am known. (1 Corinthians 13:12 KJV)

Know that There Are
Special Moments!

Not all moments are the same. Most are average or ordinary. But some are extraordinary! Most moments we forget or at least put on a shelf in our minds, to never look at again.

But there is one *very special* moment in my life that happened in the summer of 1954. A long time ago, I was in Tift County, Georgia.

The special never-to-be-forgotten moment was when I turned my head and looked back over my shoulder to see this beautiful, eye-catching girl for the first time. She was seventeen. I was nineteen. She was in a parade on a float. She has told me later that she also looked and saw me. I, too, was on the float.

No girl, female, woman, opposite-sex beauty ever caught my attention like that before or since. A long time ago, a *very special* moment.

Now, many years later, over sixty to be exact, she still catches my sight, my gaze, my attention, my mind in thought, and my heart in affections.

Reading the Bible daily helps us to be alert to see what we need to see, think what we need to think, and feel what we need to feel! *Special moments!* Especially Psalm 1 and Proverbs.

> Whoso findeth a wife findeth a good thing,
> and obtaineth favor of the Lord. (Proverbs 18:22
> KJV)

It Takes Upstream Effort

❧ ⬥ ❧

It was a very hot summer day on the Ocmulgee River. And there was my teenage brother, Larry, floating downstream on a very petite rubber inner tube, probably less than two feet wide. Amazing that it was even large enough to keep him above the red river water afloat.

But there he was, happy as could be alone, planning and completing a several-mile journey. His destination was the railroad trestle several miles downstream, then getting out of the river and walking one mile up the railroad track to our home in Abbeville, Georgia. Arriving home, he looked like a cooked lobster from the sun boiling down on him. He was wearing only his bathing suit and, of course, no sunscreen lotion in the early 1950s.

Yet, it was fun for Larry. He never gave a second thought to the danger. Possibly meeting snakes or alligators. It was simply a fun, adventurous outing for a "you don't frighten me with anything" teenage boy. That pretty much described Larry—adventurous and fun loving!

Thought. In life, it's easy, maybe even seems like fun, to float downstream. *But to accomplish any worthwhile goal*, building a business, doing a good job, marrying, raising children, growing a Christian character, or being wise in life *is an upstream effort!*

Jesus said:

> Enter by the narrow gate; for the gate is wide and the way is easy, that leads to destruction and those who enter by it are many. *For the gate is narrow and the way is hard, that leads to life, and those who find it are few.* (Matthew 7:13–14 KJV)

Read and Study the Love Chapter

❦

It was school days for me, 1947. I was in the seventh grade. Twelve years old. Ms. Murray was my teacher for all subjects. Two things I remember about that year that were different from all the other twelve years of school before college and graduate school.

One was that a friend of mine, James, and I were two of her favorite students. We ran errands for her. It felt like we were favored and trusted.

The second thing I recall that was so different was that she required all of her students every year to *memorize and recite before the entire class the thirteenth chapter of 1 Corinthians*. That is often called the *love chapter* in the Bible. To this day, when I read that love chapter, I remember Ms. Murray and the favor she gave me.

Reading the Bible daily helps us to know that *God loves all of us and wants to favor us if we listen, have faith, and follow His guide*, especially Psalm 1 and Proverbs.

> And now abideth faith, hope, charity; these three; but the greatest of these is charity. (1 Corinthians 13:13 KJV)

Remember that Simple
Can Be a Great Blessing

⤜◈⤛

There was something very special and unique about Saturday afternoon in the small town of Abbeville, Georgia, in the late 1940s and early 1950s. It was the time people came to town, especially the small farmers living out in the country. Abbeville's entire town population was no more than one thousand. The countryfolk coming to town on Saturday added likely another one hundred.

The business section of town was only two blocks long. One street. Buildings on each side. Included several grocery stores. Small ones! One theater. Two drug stores. Two banks. One barbershop. One post office.

The main thing about Saturday and the business area was, small as it was, people were crowded there, moving about, busy looking, talking, and shopping their once-a-week visit to town. You could feel the aliveness and excitement.

In the grocery stores, their shopping was simple, small amounts, and predictable. Twenty-five pounds of flour, self-rising. One or two pounds of coffee. Five or ten pounds of sugar. Four pounds of lard. Tobacco—snuff, chewing, and smoking. Some penny candy for the kids. And that's about all. The farmers grew their own vegetables and raised their own meat. Simple life!

Reading the Bible daily helps us to learn to be content with the simple and less. Not more and more! Especially Proverbs.

> Not that I speak in respect of want: for I
> have learned in whatsoever state I am, therewith
> to be content. (Philippians 4:11)

Realize Some Risks
Are Good

After growing up in South Georgia, I decided to move to New Orleans in June of 1959. I was twenty-four years old. I had been married to Gayle for only two years. She was pregnant with our first child, Linda.

I wanted to begin graduate school at New Orleans Baptist Theological Seminary. I had never lived outside of Georgia. I had no job awaiting me in New Orleans. I had only $500 in savings and expecting two paychecks of $199, each coming in July and August from teaching school.

Thus, with that situation, Gayle and I moved to a city we had never seen. I had no job. Pregnant wife. Very little money. Yet, after arriving in New Orleans, we secured an apartment. I enrolled in seminary and found a job, and Linda was born in August.

It was a very risky move! But we did it! I finished seminary in three years. Also, Dianne, our second child, was born there in 1961.

Making some risky decisions is a part of an adventuresome and meaningful life, and that is great if your lives are based on biblical principles. Wisdom.

> Remember now thy Creator in the days of thy youth, while the evil days come not, nor the years draw nigh, then thou shalt say, I have no pleasure in them. (Ecclesiastes 12:1 KJV)

Recognize How Others Bless You

⟞⟝⟞

I n 2005, Hurricane Katrina came ashore at Buras, Louisiana, which is about sixty-five miles south of New Orleans. Many people may be unaware of this finger peninsula that extends so far south of New Orleans. This peninsula is very narrow with the Mississippi River on one side and wet marshland on the other. Less than half-mile wide at places, yet it houses several small communities like Buras.

I've never been back to Buras. I can't imagine much being left. Why do I even wonder and ask the question? Gayle and I, with Linda and Dianne, lived there from 1960 to 1962. We worked in a small mission church serving French Indian people. For the two and a half years witnessing there, we had only one convert to Christ even though I spent every Saturday afternoon going door-to-door, visiting with these people in their homes, reading the Bible, and praying with them. The visible results were small.

I was a seminary student at the time, being paid $300 a month by the Home Mission Board of the SBC and the Louisiana Baptist Convention.

We lived in New Orleans but spent weekends Friday through Monday in Buras.

It was a great experience for me. Actually, it was an adventure working with these people, a mixture of French, American Indian, and African American people who spoke French and English. I enjoyed being with them, listening to them, and learning from them.

While the results, statistically only one convert in over two years of ministry, may have seemed small, hopefully the seeds planted fell on some good soil.

I'm thankful for having lived in Buras. I hope it's still there in spite of Katrina.

Lesson I learned: while you may be trying to help other people, they in fact may be even a greater blessing to you.

> Bless the Lord, O my soul: an all that is within me, bless His holy name. (Psalm 103:1 KJV)

Seize Opportune Times

꧁꧂

H is mother blurted out loudly and clearly, "I don't want him [her twenty-year-old son], making decisions that will hinder him from having a good time!"

It was a Saturday. I was in a small shotgun house, visiting a French Indian family in Buras, Louisiana. Sixty-five miles South of New Orleans, right on the Mississippi River, in 1961.

It was something I did every Saturday afternoon as a twenty-five-year-old seminary student. Visit families, read the Bible, and pray with individuals, inviting them to trust Jesus Christ as Savior and Lord.

That was the conversation going on between me and this young man when his mother suddenly entered the room and made her strong interrupting comment. Thus, that was like pouring cold water on the witnessing conversation. Shortly, I left the home.

Less than a month later, I received a phone call, informing me that that same young man had fallen overboard from a barge, in no more than seven feet of water, in the gulf and drown. They found his body weeks later.

I often wondered if that mother even remembered interrupting the conversation that I had with her son.

> Seek ye the Lord while He may be found,
> call ye upon Him while He is near. (Isaiah 55:6
> KJV)

Guard Your Heart

‿⚬⚬⚬‿

We lived in New Orleans from 1959 to 1962. The city is below sea level. So all burials are aboveground in tombs. The tombs are often attractive and well-kept. They look good on the outside, but on the inside, they are full of death. Bones. Decaying bodies.

Jesus talked about this in dealing with the Pharisees. He said to them that "you are like white-washed tombs. You may look good on the outside but inwards, you are full of dead bones." Bad within.

So the main thing, the principal factor, is not just what we *look like*, or even what we may *do* sometimes.

The main *factor* is *what am I within*. My *heart*. My *thoughts*. My *motivation. Character.* Who I am? Who are *you? Anyone of us. When no one is looking.*

Bottom line is, the only one who can truly know us is God! He knows our hearts! Our mind!

When the heart. The mind. The motivation is right and good, then the action will be good. Being within is first and foremost!

Good people may fail, but they quickly correct themselves. They are not comfortable with evil deeds.

Reading the Bible daily helps me and you to guard and keep our hearts right. The results are good deeds. Good work. Character. Integrity.

> For as he thinketh in his heart, so is he.
> (Proverbs 23:7)

Believe the Difficult May
Be the Wise Choice

෴

We were living in New Orleans, 1959–1962. I had come to the end of my seminary education. At a crossroads. I had before me two job opportunities. One was in Columbus, Georgia. One was in Carlisle, Pennsylvania. The Georgia job would be like returning home where I grew up. Near extended family. Very familiar surroundings. My parents, brothers, and sisters would all be a short distance away.

Carlisle, Pennsylvania, was North! Very North! Different culture! Different climate! Totally new! A much more-challenging job! Very difficult!

It would have been very easy to return to our comfort zone, Georgia! I chose the different place. State. Culture. Job. Climate. And much more challenging!

It was the wiser choice, and consequently, I spent with my immediate family twenty years in Pennsylvania and Maryland, 1962–1982.

I've never regretted that decision! Life changing!

Sometimes, the right decision and the wisest decision may be the most difficult and most challenging!

> In all thy ways acknowledge Him and He
> shall direct thy paths. (Proverb 3:6 KJV)

Accept It: You Can't Totally Prevent Trouble

☙◦◦◦◦❧

It was a cold winter with lots of snow in the country, near Carlisle, Pennsylvania. About 1963. We had moved there the year before.

Snow was so deep that the city had to haul it out of Carlisle by big dump truckloads.

In our own yard, out in the country, about three miles from Carlisle, the snow was two and three feet deep. Our dog couldn't walk through the snow without going out of sight. So he would jump up and out of the snow, then down out of sight into the snow, like a porpoise diving in and out of sight in the water.

That was the snowy situation when I had a wreck in our new 1962 Chevrolet. Green four-door sedan. We were all in the car: Gayle, the kids, and I. Riding out on a country road. Snow piled up at an intersection. Crossroads. I couldn't see what was coming to my left. A pile of snow ten feet high blocked my vision. So I pulled out. Another car plowed into me. No one was hurt, but the police blamed me. Took my license for three months.

Life happens no matter how hard we try. Just the way it is. Circumstances. Events. Accidents.

Jesus said:

> In the world ye shall have tribulation, but be of good cheer, I have overcome the world. (John 16:33 KJV)

Diamonds Are Nice
but Not Necessary

☙ ☙

"**I** lost my wedding ring in the barn in the hay." These were the words of my beautiful, young wife, Gayle, thirty years old. She was already the mother of our two girls and two boys. Married to me at twenty.

We lived in Carlisle, Pennsylvania, at that time. It was 1966. We had moved there from New Orleans four years before. We were renting an old two-story farmhouse, with a huge barn on the property.

Truth was, she had never received an engagement ring from me when we got married in June of 1957. Only a gold band. I could not afford an engagement ring. The only thing I owned at twenty-two years of age was a black two-door '49 Chevy. And I had a promise of a school teaching job in September, making about $200 a month.

Now fast forward to 2020. Married sixty-two years to Gayle. I've often said that she is the third generation of great women. Her mother and two grandmothers! And today, she does wear a beautiful diamond.

Reading the Bible when young definitely helps you make a good decision about marriage. As you grow old together in marriage, it helps you stay together! And love one another. With or without diamonds!

Who can find a virtuous woman, for her
price is far above rubies. (Proverbs 31:10 KJV)

Ask and Believe God
Will Lead You

❦

It was the fall of 1967. We were thinking of leaving Carlisle, Pennsylvania. Our family had gone through some rough months. Alan, two years old, had been very ill. Wayne, at birth, almost died. My back surgery had complications. So physically and emotionally, our family, Gayle and I, were tired and exhausted.

Then, out of the blue, I got this phone call from a man on the Eastern Shore of Maryland. The first thing he said was, "We need a preacher down here!" That strong voice was that of Stanley Moore from Crisfield, Maryland, a small town located on the Chesapeake Bay.

How did he get my name? How he thought or knew we might be interested in moving, I'll never know. Nevertheless, he initiated the call.

Later we learned, after moving to Crisfield, that Stanley Moore was a very assertive guy. He quickly spoke his mind yet was always positive. Truly a great person. Always encouraging to our entire family. A friend of ours till his death.

But the question I never learned was, what ignited that spark of our contact with him? What was the process that preceded and led to his first call to me saying, "We need a preacher down here."

Lesson: Some events, some introductions, some decisions, seemingly, just happen. They seem to be a mystery. Or does God lead or cause them to happen for us? *If we want God to lead us and ask Him to lead, I believe He leads us.* Think about it.

> I will instruct thee and teach thee in the way which thou shall go: I will guide thee with mine eye. (Psalm 32:8 KJV)

Don't Be Arrogant about Yourself

ᴄ✺✺ᴅ

A church member said to me, "I'm surprised to see you in a place like this." The place was a bar-restaurant, mainly a bar, but they did serve food.

My response to his statement was, "Perhaps I should come here more often" as he walked by our table on his way out.

That was the scene in 1972 as Dr. Frank Stagg, a New Testament professor, and myself, pastor of First Baptist Church, sat eating together late one evening in Crisfield, Maryland. Dr. Stagg had been my professor at New Orleans Baptist Theological Seminary years before.

I had invited him to speak at our church. I had been a pastor there since 1967. I was taking him out to eat after the evening worship service at the only place open at that hour. We were not *drinking*, just eating.

Reading the Bible daily may help us not to become arrogant, pridefully thinking we are so much better than others and at the same time giving us the wisdom to realize that drinking alcohol is not necessary to have a good time with friends!

> For I say, through the grace given to me, to every man that is among you, not to think of himself more highly than he ought to think; but to think soberly, according as God hath dealt to every man the measure of faith. (Romans 12:3 KJV)

> Wine is a mocker, strong drink is raging: and whosoever is deceived thereby is not wise. (Proverbs 20:1 KJC)

Keep Your Relationship's Current

✧⊙⊙✧

Crisfield, Maryland, the early 1970s

There I sat visiting with Tom in his home. We sat facing each other. I was in a straight chair. He was in the rocker, sitting up. Dead. He had died less than an hour before.

His wife, Carolyn, had called me immediately after he died. Before the funeral director arrived, I was there. She had asked if I would sit with him while she was busy tidying up the house. So I did.

Tom had been in the hospital. Heart trouble. Almost died a few days before. So his death was no surprise. He was in his seventies. Not well.

Since I had known Tom so well, it was not uncomfortable for me to sit with him. We had talked many times before, but now, no conversation. Just silence and my thoughts. With a dead man. A friend.

Reading the Bible daily helps you to *stay current with your relationships*. Friends and relatives. So when death comes, you have no regrets. No "I wish I had."

> A friend loveth at all times and a brother is
> born for adversity. (Proverbs 17:17 KJV)

Weep with Those Who Weep

Vietnam era: 1967–1972

With an army officer, I was walking into a business where Earl and Alice worked. Over a loudspeaker, I heard their names being called to come to the front office.

They came into the office reception area. There I stood, their pastor, with the Army Officer. Silence. Not one of the four of us had said a word when Alice, the mother of her soldier son in Vietnam, at the sight of us, immediately crumbled to the floor weeping. Her husband, the father of their son, George, kneeled beside her trying to console her. He, too, was in tears.

They knew the message! Without it being voiced! "Your son, George, twenty-five years old, has been killed in action."

A few weeks later, his body was returned to his home in Crisfield, Maryland, for burial. His casket was not permitted to be opened.

Almost nothing seems to help such grief. However, reading the Bible like Psalm 23 does bring some comfort. Hope. Faith.

> *The Lord is nigh unto them that are of a broken heart*, and saveth such as be of a contrite heart. (Psalm 34:18 KJV)

> Rejoice with them that do rejoice, and weep with them that weep. (Romans 12:15 KJV)

Listen to Your Children

∽ⓒⓖⓓ∼

S he was ten years old, standing at the top of the stairs, looking down at me. Red hair. Blue eyes. Innocent facial expression. Looking down at me as I stood at the bottom of the stairs.

Her words to me were, "Daddy, I felt God speaking to my heart tonight."

We were living in Crisfield, Maryland. It was 1969. A Sunday night about nine. We had just come home as a family from a church worship service.

At that time, we had four children. Ages ten, eight, three, and two. Two girls. Two boys. I had been trying to get them settled down to bed for about the third time. Admittedly, I was becoming frustrated as a tired, had-a-long day parent. At that moment, I heard Linda, who was ten years of age, speak to me, very tenderly, very childlike, with all the sincerity a child can speak to an earthly father, *"Daddy, I felt God speaking to my heart tonight."*

Immediately my frustration melted away. Humbled. I asked her to come back downstairs. We prayed together. Father with daughter.

Reading the Bible helps a parent to know when to speak and when not to.

> And ye fathers, provoke not your children
> to wrath: but bring them up in the nurture and
> admonition of the Lord. (Ephesians 6:4 KJV)

Recognize Amazing Faith
in Incredible Grief

He was a Baltimore City, Maryland, policeman. He asked me, a Baptist minister, "Can you help me?" Why was a policeman asking a pastor that question?

This policeman had had nine children. But when he asked me the question, his nine-year-old son had just recently drowned in the Chesapeake Bay.

So with his wife and eight remaining children following him, there they were in church on a Sunday morning, coming down the aisle to the altar, in their deep sense of grief. Sorrow. Some weeping.

Less than one month later, having made professions of faith in Christ, I baptized individually the whole family in the *Chesapeake Bay at the very same location where their nine-year-old son had drowned.* The mother had requested that!

Only by faith can a person deal with such grief.

> Yea, though I walk through the valley of the shadow of death, I will fear no evil: for Thou art with me: Thy rod and Thy staff they comfort me. (Psalm 23:4 KJV)

PS. This happened when I was pastor of Lake Shore Baptist Church in Pasadena, Maryland (1972–1982).

Learn from the Peanuts

❧

When Peanut died in 1975, we wept, my wife and I. Gayle, my wife, was the one who had chosen to bring him to our home in Maryland from South Georgia when he was a small puppy. Only a few weeks old.

Why would we weep over the death of a small, short-legged dachshund? Many people would say, "He was just a dog!"

However, to us, our family, Peanut was more than just a dog. Our boys, Alan and Wayne, were young at that time. Each wanted to take turns having Peanut sleep with them, rotating night after night.

He was cute. Coppertone in color. Like a penny. Had a personality his very own. He didn't like to be left alone. He was very social. Loved togetherness with the family. Loved to be held. Loved to be loved.

Reading the Bible daily teaches us a lot about loving one another.

Being together. Social. We can also learn a lot from little animals like Peanut.

> And God made the beast of the earth after his kind, and cattle after their kind, and everything that creepeth upon the earth after his kind: and God saw that it was good. (Genesis 1:25 KJV)

> Beloved, if God so loved us, we ought also to love one another. (1 John 4:11 KJV)

Look Forward, Not Backward!

಄ᎣᏀᏁ

O ne of the problems that I confess to having lots of trouble with through the years is the tendency to look back. Wondering, second questioning myself, "Did I make the right decision?" Often it would have to do with a job change and a geographical move for the family.

This anxiety would haunt me even after I had prayed earnestly before making the decision, sincerely asking God for wisdom and guidance.

Some people call similar feelings, "buyer's remorse." Mine wasn't exactly like that. Mine would torture me worse! For hours, days, even years! Looking back over my shoulder.

Looking back trying to rewrite your history is an impossibility! *We can hopefully learn from our past. Do better looking forward. But change it? No! Never!*

Accept it. Stay in the present. Today, the now is all we can live. We can't relive any yesterdays! I tell myself!

Reading the Bible daily. Psalm 1 and Proverbs help me live today. At least to be better at it! I hope it will help you.

> Brethren, I count not myself to have appre-
> hended: but this one thing I do, forgetting those
> things which are behind and reaching forth unto
> those things which are before. (Philippians 3:13
> KJV)

Realize Understanding
May Come Later

∿◦⊙◦∿

This past weekend (March 2021), I made a quick decision to drive to Maryland by myself. No escort. No one to help me drive up Interstate 95 North through South Carolina, North Carolina, Virginia, and on into Maryland. The traffic was unbelievably heavy. Dangerous.

My goal at the age of eighty-five years was to visit two places where we had lived from 1967 until 1982. Five years in Crisfield, Maryland, and ten years in Pasadena, Maryland, suburban Baltimore.

When I left my job as a pastor of Lake Shore Baptist Church in 1982 in Pasadena, I did so with a lot of grief. Have second-guessed myself many times through the years of my decision to move.

But on my recent trip, alone, I looked at the place, the situation, perhaps with a better and more realistic understanding; considered my years that have flown by; and came to a better understanding of my past and my present.

My conclusion was that complete understanding or even a healthy understanding of life often comes to us in retrospect as we look back. Just maybe God had seen what I couldn't see. And perhaps it was His hand that moved me. Maybe I wasn't alone in the decision back then.

Nevertheless, *I now have a better understanding of my past. Reading the Bible, especially Psalms and Proverbs, helps us to understand better day by day.*

> For now we see through a glass darkly: but then face to face: Now I know in part; but then shall I know even as also I am known. (1 Corinthians 13:12 KJV)

Have an Acceptable Heart

Questioning myself, regarding my own heart, spiritually. What kind of heart is acceptable to God? Jesus said, "Thou shalt love the Lord thy God with all thy heart, and with all thy soul, and with all thy mind, and with all thy strength" (Mark 12:30 KJV).

That's a very big and very tall order, commandment, straight from Jesus. No half a heart or any partial will be acceptable. The whole heart and only the whole!

King David, certainly, as history reports, was not perfect. He committed some bad stuff. Adultery. Murder. Cover-up.

But according to Psalm 32, David confessed, turned from his sin, and humbled himself. He cried out to God for forgiveness! *That humble broken heart was and is what God wants from us as acceptable. Not perfect. Acceptable!*

Reading the Bible daily helps us to gain and retain a heart acceptable to God. Psalm 1 and Proverbs especially.

> The Lord is nigh unto them that are of a broken heart; and saveth such as be of a contrite heart. (Psalm 34:18 KJV)

Tell Loved Ones that
You Love Them

෴

"*Warren, Tom and I have always loved you.*" Those were pretty strong and very meaningful words given to me by my mother-in-law, Mama Fay. Tom was her husband and my father-in-law. My wife's parents.

Even more interesting was that Mama Fay said these words to me as we arrived back at her home immediately after my father-in-law's funeral in 1983.

I've often wondered how it must feel to be a mother and a father with only two children, one being their only daughter. Then one day, a young guy, as I was at twenty-two years old, comes and takes her away. She, Gayle, was only twenty years old when we were married in 1957.

Anyway, when my mother-in-law, Mama Fay, said those words to me, they were powerful and reassuring. I've always thought she felt that way, but sometimes *words are extra special gifts!* Even in times and places when you least expect them.

> Pleasant words are as a honeycomb, sweet to the soul and health to the bones. (Proverbs 16:24)

Thank God for Small Pleasures

❧❦❧

My grandmother Burnham lived to be ninety-six years of age. She lived longer than her only husband, my grandfather, Dolph Burnham, by several years. When she married him, she was only a teenager. He was thirty.

The story told me was that her father actually *gave her* to my grandfather to wed. Sort of like a *fixed marriage*. They lived in Dodge County, near Rhine, Georgia, on a farm.

He was a rural mail carrier and a farmer. They had twelve children. Nine lived to be adults. The youngest was born in 1933. The oldest, my father, was born in 1911. All grew up in a house with no electricity. No indoor plumbing. No running water. Just a well. And an outhouse. Three bedrooms in the house. One for the girls. One for the boys. One for my grandparents.

Yet in spite of a very tough, austere, frugal life, Grandmother was a devout Christian!

She had one secret pleasure; she kept hidden, only for herself, peppermint candy!

> Although the fig tree shall not blossom, neither shall fruit be in the vines; the labor of the olive shall fail, and the fields shall yield no meat; the flock shall be cut off from the fold, and there shall be no herd in the stalls; *yet I will rejoice in the Lord, I will joy in the God of my Salvation.* (Habakkuk 3:17–18 KJV)

Don't Be Arrogant

I had the pleasure of having in essence two whole careers. Over thirty years as a Baptist minister or pastor. Served in Pennsylvania, Maryland, Georgia, and Louisiana.

Then after those meaningful years, I was pleased to work and listen as a psychotherapist for twenty-eight years. Retired at eighty-three.

Nevertheless, two of the things I often said to young couples about to be married were "Can or will you tell me three of your weaknesses? Then, tell me three of your strengths."

Interesting was the fact that most people, especially during the 1955–1988 era, had no problem relating their weaknesses to me. But stumbled for words in sharing anything good about themselves.

Whether that would be a problem in our present era, I'm not sure. Some today seem arrogant. Unaware of any need for improvement in growth. Already know it all! May already have it all!

Point to consider. It's okay and good to be self-aware of your strengths, but overly arrogant people are usually totally unteachable.

Humility is a very important characteristic to own. Humble people usually are eager to listen and eager to learn. They know that they may become more educated but still never know it all!

> When pride cometh, then cometh shame: but with the lowly is wisdom. (Proverbs 11:2 KJV)

Be Careful with Your Words

❧

He was only twelve years old when he said to himself, "He will never say to me again the things that he has said in the past in front of other people."

Now, thirty years later, he was describing the scene and his experience of finding the dead body of his father.

As he spoke, now a forty-plus-year-old man, tears were streaming down his face. There were only three people in the room. Me, himself, and his wife. He was not a talkative kind of a guy. In fact, he was more of an introvert. His words were so soft and few, but his tears were so obvious. Physically, he was a very big man. Tall. Heavyset.

But now the truth was finally coming out. Years later. From his past. He had been the first to find his father. Dead. And he was not saddened by the event and sight! His response was a relief!

He never said that his father physically abused him. It was WORDS. Negative words. ONLY words. Putting him down words.

Words can be extremely powerful. Good words. Bad words. Words can destroy, or words can build and strengthen.

Reading the Bible daily, especially the Psalms and Proverbs, can help us to gain the wisdom to make our words few and good and encouraging.

> Death and life are in the power of the tongue: and they that love it shall eat the fruit thereof. (Proverbs 18:21 KJV)

Give Your Spouse Attention and Affection

❧◉❧

She said, "I sleep naked." As she said those words, her emotions came through also. Loud and clear! Tearful eyes and anger in her voice. She intended them to be heard and felt. She was not glad to say those words in some sort of lighthearted or humorous manner. She was seriously and painfully upset, talking about her marriage. Her husband also was seated in the room as she spoke. He was somber and droopy eyed. He heard her with no denial and almost no response.

What message did she want to be heard? It was clear; her husband showed her no affection. No attention. Such had been the truth for most of their marriage, in spite of her every effort to get both, especially the affection, from the only man on earth ethically and morally that she was supposed to receive it from.

As a therapist, a Christian counselor, I have heard many hours of similar stories. Why? Is the husband having an affair? Having his needs met somewhere else? Looking at pornography?

Often, the answer was never given. But the problem of a neglected, young attractive wife was always explosively obvious. And the marriage would be hanging by a flimsy, weak thread. Often the thread broke.

> So ought men to love their wives as their own bodies. He that loveth his wife loveth himself. (Ephesians 5:28 KJV)

Give Your Heart to God, Your Marriage, Your Work

Something I've thought about for some time now. I believe there is a difference between the mind, the heart, and the soul. Our soul is what lives on after our heart and brain have stopped. Brain-dead. Heart stopped beating, but our soul lives on for eternity. Later at some point, I believe we are also given a new body to house our soul. How soon, I'm not sure. But definitely, a new body for believers in Christ.

Then there is our heart and mind for our here and now. I believe our minds can tell our hands and feet what to do and where to go. But our heart is separate. Our heart cannot be totally controlled by our mind.

For instance, we may be told or commanded by our minds to do a job with our hands and feet, and we obey. But our heart may not be in it.

Our heart is a separate entity. *Our heart is the depth of our being. Our inner self. Our heart is what God wants. Not just the performance of our hands and feet.* If our heart is given to God, our hands and feet will act right. We will do the work, whatever it is, as He wants us to.

I can recall in my past work that I've had to do. Jobs. Assignments. Some I did with my hands and feet performing, but not with my heart. *Just going through the motion!* Others with *all my heart!* Difference!

When your heart's in it, there is always love. Question. Does your relationship to God, your marriage, and your work, have your heart? Or just going through the motions?

> For the Lord seeth not as a man seeth: for man looketh on the outward appearance, but the Lord looketh on the heart. (1 Samuel 16:7 KJV)

Stay in Touch with Good People

✑⟨⟨⟨⟩⟩⟩✑

"**H**ey, Warren. I have a joke to tell you!" That was the opening line from the voice on my cell phone. The person calling me was a friend I have known for many, many years. We stay in touch by phone. He calls me. I call him. He lives in Maryland. I live in Georgia. Hundreds of miles apart. His name is Wayne. He and his wife have a beautiful relationship. The reason I describe it as beautiful is that the romance between them is so obvious. Both seem happy within themselves individually and so pleased to be together.

Although they have been through very heartbreaking tragedies together, they still are so full of hope and faith. And love! You can see it in their eyes and hear it in their voices.

Their tragedies include her stroke at an early age and the accidental death of a grandchild.

People like that, still so full of life and love, are good for us to know and stay in touch with!

> That thou mayest walk in the way of good men, and keep the paths of the righteous. (Proverbs 2:20 KJV)

Realize Silence Is Often Golden

∽৩৩৩৩৩৩

S he looked me straight in the eye. Eye to eye, she said to me, *"I sometimes think things, but I don't say them."* As she spoke, she pointed to her head with her right hand with a very serious expression on her face. She was seated only about two or three feet across the table from me.

Here comes the punch line, the startling fact. *She was only four years old.* My granddaughter. *Amy (2004).*

What brought such a thought to her mind? The situation was that she had just been corrected about some of her behavior. My wife, her grandmother, had been the disciplinarian. Whatever it was that Amy had been corrected for, she didn't like it. Disagreeing with her grandmother, she looked directly at me with a puzzled look and slightly rolled her eyes. Then she made that statement, *"Sometimes I think things, but I don't say them."*

My response, an adult to a four-year-old, wondering how in the world did she come upon such *wisdom* at four years of age, was *"that's very wise thinking!"* Just because you think some things doesn't mean you have to say it! Silence is in fact often golden, if not diamond!

Listening and thinking wisely should always precede speaking and sometimes should stop us from speaking at all!

Reading the Bible daily thoughtfully, *especially Proverbs helps, us to gain wisdom* on *when to speak and when to keep silent.*

He that hath knowledge spareth his words.
And he that shutteth his lips is esteemed a man of
understanding. (Proverbs 17:28 KJV)

Accept and Deal with Your Regrets

❧

"Your brother, Larry, is dead. He died of a heart attack." Those were the words I heard over the phone that caused me to fall to my knees, weeping, in grief!

It was 2010. Larry, my brother, was only seventy-four years old. He was living in Perry, Georgia, with his second wife. He was only sixteen months younger than me.

Admittedly, we had not been that close since I had left home at eighteen. But growing up, it was quite different. Almost like twins. Going everywhere together. Doing things together. He was the first of our five siblings to die. Three brothers. Two sisters.

I've often wondered why his death hit me so hard, like a flash of lightning. Since we had not been close since finishing high school.

The grief was twofold. We had been extremely close growing up and extremely distant as adults.

Family life and memories, past and present, often collide in our minds like a storm.

Reading the Bible helps us to maintain or regain some sense of comfort and calm as we struggle with our grief and regrets, especially Psalm 23 and Proverbs.

> Let not your heart be troubled: ye believe in
> God believe also in Me. (John 14:1 KJV)

Confess and Find Forgiveness

‿◦◎◦‿

As mischievous children, we didn't know that it would catch fire so quickly and burn so fast, but it did! We tried as youngsters, the three of us under the ages of eleven, to put out the fire. And we thought we did, but apparently, we didn't.

Playing inside a warehouse full of cottonseed, we saw these large webs of dust hanging from the ceiling. As curious and crazy-acting kids, we wondered if it would burn. We learned quickly. The webs of dust caught fire like gasoline!

Sirens and firetrucks later that day said to us, "You didn't put the fire out." Nevertheless, we never went back to assess the damages!

Until years later, as an adult in my twenties, I thought about it intensely. Feeling much-delayed guilt, I went to the owner of the seed house. Confessed! His reply was, "Warren, if I knew for sure that I could clean out that warehouse like that fire did, I would set fire to it every year." *Forgiven. My guilt is gone!*

Reading the Bible daily may not completely spare us of crazy, stupid behavior in our youth, or anytime, but *it helps us to confess and find forgiveness and not to repeat it!* Especially Psalm 1 and Proverbs.

> If we confess our sins, He is faithful and
> just to forgive us our sins, and to cleanse us of all
> unrighteousness. (1 John 1:9 KJV)

Appreciate the Ordinary

❧❦❧

We were flying high over the Grand Canyon sometime in the 1990s in a very small propeller airplane. It was one of those planes with a maximum capacity of about ten or less. It was a hot summer day. We were visiting Las Vegas and heard about the plane rides over the Grand Canyon. We thought that would be an enjoyable, meaningful, and learning experience to see the Grand Canyon from above.

It was a miserable mistake! Bad decision! Not what we thought it might be! The petite plane was extremely LOUD! It was a rough ride! The plane shook like a feather in a windstorm.

Sick at my stomach would not even come close to describing my feelings. I felt sick all over. Stomach. Head. Nerves. Scared. And I had paid money for this!

Finally, arriving back at the airport with my feet on the ground, out of the clouds, felt like a heaven-sent moment!

Reading the Bible daily helps us to *appreciate the ordinary! The simple! The just-having-your-feet-on-the-ground days!* No high-in-the-sky feelings!

> Better is a handful with quietness than both hands full with travail and vexation of spirit. (Ecclesiastes 4:6 KJV)

> Be still and know that I am God. (Psalm 46:10 KJV)

Memorize Psalm 27 Verse 1

లంల

F lat of my back, after back surgery, a spinal fusion. In Carlisle, Pennsylvania, Hospital, 1966, thirty-one years of age. Questioning myself, "Did I do the right thing?" Having the surgery. Second-guessing myself. "Was it absolutely necessary? Would I be able to walk again?"

I was not permitted to get out of bed for fourteen days. Not at all. For nothing! Complications set in. Hospitalized for twenty-one days.

Didn't feel like praying. Couldn't sit up to hold a Bible to read.

However, I had memorized Psalm 27:1. So I repeated it to myself over and over daily. Some people call that meditating.

Whether that was what helped to heal me physically and help me emotionally, I don't know. *But I do know it brought me great comfort and encouragement then and still does today.* I recommend it to you daily!

> The Lord is my light and my salvation: whom shall I fear. The Lord is the strength of my life of whom shall I be afraid. (Psalm 27:1 KJV)

Relax Even in the Rain

Today, looking out my kitchen windows, I can see several squirrels eating in my backyard. In the rain! The rain doesn't seem to bother them at all, and not one of them has an umbrella. Eating undisturbed in the rain with no evidence of worry, with no shelter of any kind. They seem totally concentrating on eating.

Also, there are two or three birds of different sorts joining them. The birds and squirrels seem to be okay with the presence of the others. Though so different. No conflicts. No exclusions!

Would it not be a good thing if people, human beings, all created in the image of God could be so relaxed! So accepting of one another. So inclusive, not worried, and not disturbed by the rains of life that are inevitable. Even without an umbrella. Faith is the answer.

Reading the Bible daily helps us to have more faith. Helps us not to be so worried or distracted by the hard rains of life that are inevitable.

> Thou wilt keep him in perfect peace whose mind is stayed on thee: because he trusteth in thee. (Isaiah 26:2 KJV)

Touch One Another

❦

For the most part, it happens every night 365 days a year, my crawling into bed with my wife. Like I say, almost every night for sixty-two years, we have slept together. The only thing that keeps it from happening is maybe illness or if one of us is out of town.

If we sleep together, there is touching, physical touching. Sometimes snuggling. Also, during the waking hours, when one of us leaves the house on an errand or whatever, there is a hug, maybe a kiss to say, "Goodbye, see you later."

Why is this so important? Listening to folks in the privacy of my office, as a counselor for almost thirty years, I was amazed at the social distancing. Lack of touching between married people—husband and wife, male and female. Sadly, that meant so much loneliness! And loneliness and sadness were always expressed. Heard by me and others!

Physical touch. Hugs. Kisses. Intimacy is a crying hunger! Needed between husband and wife.

Reading the Bible daily teaches the need of physically loving, touching between husband and wife, especially the Song of Solomon and Proverbs 5:18–19 (KJV).

> So ought men to love their wives as their own bodies. He that loveth his wife loveth himself. (Ephesians 5:28 KJV)

Respond Kindly to God's Kindness

"Why is God so kind to us?" Amy asked me on December 7, 2008. She was eight years old. Admittedly, I didn't come up with a quick answer. Personally startled by such a question from an eight-year-old and also her being my granddaughter.

Of course, maybe I shouldn't have been so surprised because she is the one who also astonished me when she was about six. At that time, I asked her, "What must we do to go to heaven?" She quickly responded, "We must die."

Now at the age of twenty, she gives evidence of being serious about her relationship with God. Her behavior gives testimony that she is a believer. A Christian. Her genuine faith in Jesus Christ.

Anyway, back to her question, "Why is God so kind to us?" Think about that. However, *don't take His kindness for granted.* His kindness is for now. *There will be a reckoning if a person rejects his kindness.*

> Many sorrow shall be to the wicked: but he that trusteth in the Lord, mercy shall compass him about. (Psalm 32:10 KJV)

Know When to
Say "No"

⤚⊙⊙⊙⤙

A good friend called me just a few days ago and asked, "Will you do a favor for me?."

I immediately responded, "Sure. Yes." Really before I found out what his request was. Since he is a good friend and, in the past, has been helpful to me, without even thinking, I was saying, "Yes."

A few days later, having had time to reconsider the request. I was thinking, *How is the best way to handle this? What's the wise way to deal with it?*

I changed my approach to the situation and favor request. My conclusion wasn't a total *no*, but it certainly wasn't a quick *yes* as he had requested.

How about that issue of how and when to say, "No" or "Not now" or "Maybe later." Persons like me, often wanting to please people, regardless of the cost, have trouble saying no, especially to a friend.

But it's important to learn when to say "No" to friends. Family. Even to yourself. Listen carefully first to the request. Think about it before you say "Yes." The answer may be "No." Regardless of who may be asking. *Trying always to please everyone is not necessarily a wise motivation.*

Reading the Bible daily, especially Proverbs, helps you to know when to say "No."

> He that answereth a matter before he heareth it is folly and shame unto him. (Proverbs 18:13 KJV)

Know that God Will
Hold Your Hand

⊱⊰⊱⊰⊱

> For God has not given us a spirit of fear;
> but of power and of love and of a sound mind. (2
> Timothy 1:7 KJV)

I'm not sure when this verse of scripture became a favorite of mine. I had it printed on my professional stationery. Frequently for years, it has been on the front row of my mind, my thoughts.

Fear is not an uncommon factor in life. Fear of failure. Fear of the future. Fear of persons. Fear of health. Fear of life itself. Fear of death. We humans often tend to be afraid. But the Bible over and over records God saying to us, *"Fear not. Let not your heart be troubled. Be not dismayed."*

Years ago, when our oldest daughter, Linda, was only about five or six years old, we lived in Carlisle, Pennsylvania. It was a Sunday evening, leaving our church building. Just the two of us, she and I were about to walk out. Lights were out. Darkness suddenly surrounded us. She immediately began to cry. Fear of the dark! Quickly, I reached down and took her hand. Her crying ceased. The darkness was still there.

The difference was she had her father's hand.

Reading the Bible daily helps us to realize and be often reminded of our Heavenly Father's willingness to hold our hand even in our darkest days.

> For the Lord thy God will hold thy right
> hand, saying unto thee, Fear not; I will help thee.
> Fear thou not; for I am with thee: be not dis-

mayed; for I am thy God: I will strengthen thee; yea, I will help thee; yea I will uphold thee with the right hand of my righteousness. (Isaiah 41:10 and 13 KJV)

Appreciate the Value
of Good Friends

꧁◌◌꧂

After their three-day visit, they left this morning at seven-twenty to return to their home in Pennsylvania. Mother and daughter. Mary and Beverly. Mary is eighty-four years of age. Beverly sixty. Both longtime friends of Gayle and myself. We became friends over fifty years ago. 1962. Known them ever since. Kept in touch by phone and personal visits although lived hundreds of miles apart.

We met them, their families, in church. It has been our like faith, Christian values, and love that have kept us together through the years. Together in friendship, though not by geography.

We tell a lot about ourselves by the friends we make. And the friends we keep. The friends one makes can help to make or break one.

Reading the Bible daily definitely helps us to make and keep good friends, the kind that encourages and strengthens us in positive ways throughout life. *Read Psalm 1 and Proverbs.*

> Wise friends make you wise, but you hurt yourself by going around with fools. (Proverbs 13:20 CEV)

> He that walketh with wise men shall be wise: but a companion of fools shall be destroyed. (Proverbs 13:20 KJV)

Be Careful How You Spend
Your Younger Years

~~~

W e lived near Baltimore in Pasadena, Maryland, but I was going to school in Philadelphia. Once a week, I had to commute between the cities. Driving. I was attending Eastern Baptist Theological Seminary, working on a doctor of ministry degree. That was during the years between 1972 and 1982 while I was pastor of Lake Shore Baptist Church. The church was in the midst of a major building program. The church was borrowing and spending so much money that it caused me some anxiety. But the building committee, the deacons, and the church body seemed to have no anxiety, so we did it. Borrowed the money. Built the beautiful new sanctuary with no problem.

But with so much involved, so many irons in the fire, so to speak, including being married and father of four children, all at home, including two teenagers, it was a busy time!

So to find study time, the only time I could carve out of my daily schedule was 10:00 p.m. until 2:00 a.m.

I was young, and my energy level was adequate. Much greater than older years.

Funny how one remembers small pieces of the puzzle of life. I recall often driving into Philadelphia in the early morning, stopping at a red light, and someone would rush up to my car window selling hot bagels!

It's a blessing to have meaningful memories of one's younger days. It's a fact, *you're only young once! Use your time and energy wisely!*

> *Remember now Thy Creator in the days of thy youth*, while the evil days come not, for the years draw nigh, when thou shalt say, I have no pleasure in them. (Ecclesiastes 12:1 KJV)

Thank God for
Your Places

ంకుఁ

S he, Gayle, asked me, "Do you want to go by our old house again?"
We were just out riding around.

Very casual, I responded, "Yes."

So we drove by our former residence. We lived there for twenty-eight years, 1990–2018. The longest time that either of us lived
anywhere. Even living at home, as children, with our parents, our
stay was no more than twenty years.

So why did she ask the question? Why did I say, "Yes"? There
are many memories we made there. Watched our children and
grandchildren swim in our pool there. Spent many fleeting moments
watching large catfish swim in the shallow water's edge of the pond
behind our house.

There we also learned to love, then adopt a stray neighborhood
cat, Raven. He was ours for years before one fatal day in his older
years when he ran out in front of a vehicle and was killed. Raven was
buried there.

We mourned his death.

So when Gayle asked me the question regarding driving by our
old house. It was more than just a house.

Places we've lived in became more to us than just wood and
stone. They hold memories. They became part of our lives. They
remind us of our past. *Places live and breathe with your joys and sad
times.*

Thank God for the *places* in your past, your present, and your
future!

Jesus said:

> In My Father's house are many mansions:
> if it were not so I would have told you. I go to
> prepare a place for you. (John 14:2 KJV)

Make Important Rock-Solid Decisions, Not Like Sandcastles

୧୬୭ଡ଼ୟ

S everal times in the summertime, Gayle and I have visited Destin, Florida, on the Gulf Coast. A couple of times, we took Amy and Cara, our granddaughters, with us. They always, as teenagers, added fun to our trip to see the ocean and walk on the beach.

Part of the fun would be watching children build sandcastles. They would build them, then the ocean tide would gradually overtake and wash them away.

Often, I've thought and compared some decisions to sandcastles. Decisions seemingly so fun to make must not last or survive the inevitable ocean tides of life.

Marriage, saying, "I do." All smiles. Feeling so in love. But the tides of life gradually wash it away.

Also, like a person walking the aisle of some church, saying, "Yes, I want to be a Christian." Be baptized. Put my name on the church role. Then the tides of life, temptations, and the like wash away that decision. Like a sandcastle. Like it never even happened.

Some decisions are extremely important. Like faith in Christ. Committing your life to follow Him. Also, marriage. These decisions should be *like the Rocky Mountains*. Unmovable by the waves and tides of life. *Not like sandcastles.*

Reading the Bible daily helps us to make rock-solid decisions. Unmovable! Joshua said to Israel "Choose this day whom ye will serve." But as for me and my house, we will serve the Lord (Joshua 24:15 KJV).

> Your love is faithful, Lord, and even the clouds in the sky can depend on you. Your decisions are always fair. They are firm like mountains, deep like the sea. (Psalm 36:5–6 CEV)

Keep Learning, Seeking Wisdom

❧◦◎◦☙

There I was fifty-three years of age. The oldest person in my class. The year was 1988. I was a student at the University of Georgia, working on a master's in social work degree. I already had earned a bachelor's degree, a master's degree in theology, and a doctor of ministry degree from Eastern Baptist Seminary in Philadelphia. Already spent nine years beyond high school.

Gayle and I have, since 1988, gone to so many places for my continuing education. Vancouver, British Colombia; Montreal; Chicago; Las Vegas; Hawaii; San Diego; Atlanta; and other places.

Then on top of that, Gayle and our kids accuse me of reading a lot. Many books are in our home library. I usually buy books, rather than borrow them from a library. One reason for that is, I like to write notes in the book, always underlining. Often reading them again and again.

One major point for me to constantly be aware of is my need to learn more and admit to myself how little I really know.

Another point is, I've always enjoyed being in the classroom. It was fun for me to be, in Athens, back in school at the age of fifty-three.

> Wise men lay up knowledge. (Proverbs 10:14 KJV)

> Give instruction to a wise man, and he will be yet wiser: teach a just man and he will increase in learning. (Proverbs 9:9 KJV)

Know that You Are Important

~~~~

One day, I was listening to the CEO of one of the hospitals in Augusta. He said, "You know if I didn't show up this morning, I would be hardly missed, but if the housekeeping personnel, cleaning crew, didn't show up, they would definitely be missed!"

What was he saying with that comment? Oftentimes, we over-label or underlabel the importance of a job or a position. We think, thus, that some people are very important! Some are not!

Not really a wise thing to do. In an organization like a hospital or a business, every person, every job is important. Every person. Every job has value and worth. You are important regardless of your job title.

You probably have heard that one small screw on a spaceship, if not placed or done correctly, can cause the whole flight to fail.

So is that guy, the one responsible for that screw, less important than the astronaut for a successful flight? *For a successful business, every person is important!* Every job. If you want the best. Not just the good. Or the better. If your goal is the best. Excellence. Success.

It takes wise people! Doing their job! Every day! Realizing that each person is extremely important! Absolutely necessary!

> *Whatsoever thy hand findeth to do, do it with thy might*; for there is no work, nor device, nor knowledge, nor wisdom in the grave, whither thou goest. (Ecclesiastes 9:10 KJV)

> Nay, much more those members of the body, which seem to be more feeble are necessary. (1 Corinthians 12:22 KJV)

Hope toward God

It was after the election in November 2020. I was greatly disappointed and disheartened by the announced results of the presidential election, between Donald Trump and Biden. I likely shared the feelings of over seventy million Americans.

Life is like that. It's not uncommon for life to hand us circumstances and situations that we have personally, absolutely no power to change.

During these gloomy days of November 2020, reading the Bible, I was encouraged and reminded *not to give up hope.*

The apostle Paul said that *hope* was one of the foundations of the Christians' faith. He speaks of "faith, hope, and love. These three" (1 Corinthians 13:13).

Paul had that ability *anchored in his heart, soul, and mind to never give up hope.* It's a great lesson to learn. A great part of character to have and to hold on to.

Paul said:

> And have hope toward God. (Acts 24:15 KJV)

> Thou art my hiding place and my shield: I hope in thy Word. (Psalm 119:114 KJV)

Accept What You Can't Control or Change

There is a "must factor" in life that we must accept for our own well-being whether we like it or not. There is a difference between my ability to *influence* and my ability to control. There are some things I just learn to accept as being beyond my ability to control or change. That's just the way some things are, and I must learn to live with them. That is, *accept them.*

The climate. My total environment. Many circumstances. My age. Death. My past. The behavior of other people. Even my own family. Children. Grandchildren.

I can't control them. So I must just learn to live with them the best I can with God's help. Not to accept them is to die within. My heart and soul diminishes, shrinks, shrivels up, becomes lifeless, and almost ceases to exist.

But the other is possible. It takes effort and hard work to keep on living.

To thrive. To stay fully alert, alive, to truly live abundantly. Realizing *God is still alive and present to help me and us. Therefore, pray. Look up. Think about these scriptures.*

> God is our refuge and strength, a very present help in trouble. (Psalm 46:1 KJV)

> I have learned, in whatsoever state I am, therewith to be content. (Philippians 4:11 KJV)

> Christ gives me the strength to face anything. (Philippians 4:13 CEV)

Use Common Sense:
Be Self-Controlled

ᴄ☙☽ᴥ

There I stood in a courtroom in Gainesville, Georgia. I was the only one of the guilty folks there with a coat and tie. The others were a mixture of seemingly poorer people, not well-dressed. One thing we all had in common was that we all had broken the law. All were traffic violations. The fines varied, and most were unable to pay their fines, thus placed on parole or something.

My time came for the vocal announcement made loud enough for all to hear. Embarrassed. Shamed. Felt like hiding my face and running out! Then the judge, or whoever he was, said, "Your fine is $350, Mr. Burnham! We lowered the speed numbers, but you'll have to pay the full amount." No argument. I said nothing. Just handed the person at a nearby table, with his hand out, the cash.

What had happened was a few weeks before I was driving near Gainesville. Four-lane highway. Driving my Lexus, an LS400. 1993 model. Only owned it for a week or so. Bought from JH Lexus. I was speeding. Over eighty miles per hour. Don't even recall what the limit was. Nevertheless, it cost me $350 for a traffic violation! Broke the law!

Less than a year later, I gave the car to one of my sons. Subconsciously, I think I blamed the car for my $350 fine. Smooth, easy driving!

When we break physical laws, not taking care of our bodies, we pay. *When we break moral or spiritual laws, we pay! Wrong behavior costs!*

> Be not deceived: God is not mocked: for whatsoever a man soweth, that shall he also reap. (Galatians 6:7 KJV)

Realize the Earth Is a Gift from God

❦

Monday, May 13, 2019, Gayle and I were in Destin, Florida, on the white sandy beach. It was a sunny and cloudy day. Everything, including ourselves and the weather, felt calm, quiet, and relaxed. We were seated under one of the blue umbrellas for the beach only.

Needless to say, we were on no rigid schedule. No urgent demands on our minds. All we were doing was facing the ocean, observing the soft white caps, gently splashing toward our feet. People all around. Seagulls here and there. Little kids and grown adults building sand-castles. Some lying exposed to the sun, seeking tanned skin. Others like us, hiding from the sun under the umbrellas.

But for all, the young and the old, there was the gift of the ocean, the breeze, the sun, and the sand. Taking it all into our minds, our bodies, our souls, and our spirits.

Thought. God has given us a beautiful place to live. The earth. We need to thank Him for it and not mess it up.

> In the beginning God created the heaven and the earth. And God saw everything that He had made, and behold it was very good. (Genesis 1:1 and 31 KJV)

Be Kind and Be Quiet

A few days ago, I was having some very serious anxiety about a family meeting. Kids and grandkids were involved. Everyone concerned is grown. They've all seen and heard from me many times for many years.

Nevertheless, I was so anxious I was up at 3:30 a.m., worrying about the get-together. All the time rehearsing and detailing in my mind what I was to say. Trying to explain myself and so forth. All going on in mind, causing anxiety to increase more and more. I thought. I prayed. Then suddenly, the thought came to my mind. From God or from my best wisdom or just common sense. To myself, I said, *"Just be kind and be quiet!"* That's all you need to do. No speech to remember. No speech to be said. Just be kind and be quiet.

Often, is that not a very good guideline to follow? After you have already said so much to your immediate family, your kids especially, and maybe to others, it's just best to say nothing more. Just be kind and be quiet. Save your breath.

Don't waste your breath. Best to just be kind and be quiet. They already know what you're thinking.

> *And be ye kind* one to another, tenderhearted, forgiving one another, even as God for Christ's sake hath forgiven you. (Ephesians 4:32)

Reading the Bible daily, especially Proverbs, helps us to know when to just be kind and be quiet.

> And the high priest arose and said unto him, Answerest thou nothing... *But Jesus held his peace.* (Matthew 26:62–63 KJV)

To everything there is a season...a time to keep silence, and a time to speak. (Ecclesiastes 3:1, 7 KJV)

And be ye kind one to another. (Ephesians 4:32 KJV)

Trust Your Encourager
and Comforter

⸙⸙⸙

One of the most powerful and meaningful words in the New Testament is the word that is translated *comforter*. In the original language, Greek, the word is *parákletos*. It means the *Holy Spirit* that is called along beside us. To help us, to encourage us, to be with us, to be our advocate, and to actually live within us.

Really *God's gift of Himself to us as believers as people of faith and followers of Jesus Christ. Wherever we may be.*

At the graveside of a loved one.

In the hospital room or intensive care unit, facing possible or probable death.

In the midst of a broken relationship between husband and wife. Or parent and child. Friends. Neighbor. Relative.

God's promise is to *be with* us, beside us, to help us when life seems to *make no sense*. When we don't understand. When we have no answers. Or when we do have the answer, which screams, "It's all your fault! You brought it on yourself."

> The Lord of Hosts is with us; the God of Jacob is our refuge. (Psalm 46:7)

> For this God is our God forever and ever: *He will be our guide even unto death.* (Psalm 48:14 KJV)

Jesus said:

> I will pray the Father, and He shall give you
> another Comforter that He may abide with you
> forever. (John 14:16 KJV)

Don't Worry

Worry can be like a vicious animal eating up our energy—our physical and emotional and mental energy. It can attack us at night or early in the morning or all day long. It seems to have no respect of time or place, age, or person, the rich or the poor.

The fact that thousands of Americans *a year* commit suicide indicates that there are mental hurricanes going on in the minds of so many.

The fact that numerous veterans of all branches of our military commit suicide in our country *every day* gives evidence that they have no mental peace.

The sad thing about worry is that it *accomplishes absolutely nothing.*

Regardless of how much we spin the wheels of our minds worrying, we get nowhere. Somehow we know that, so why do we do it?

Reading the Bible daily, *Psalm 23 and Psalm 121*, will definitely help us not to worry and to *replace worry with faith. Faith in God.*

> Heaviness in the heart of man maketh it stoop, but a good word maketh it glad. (Proverbs 12:25 KJV)

> Rest in the Lord and wait patiently for Him. (Psalm 37:7 KJV)

Count Your Blessings

It was midmorning. Gayle and I had just read a devotional and had prayer together. And I had read some of the morning newspaper on August *21, 2021*, when I said, *"My problems are at zero."* Compared to so many circumstances and others' situations, I have no problems.

I had read of the massive killings in Afghanistan of innocent people. And thought of the horrible situations going on at the Southern border of our United States.

Then I read of a local minister having just learned of her cancer.

Earlier in the morning, admittedly, my mind had been troubled and preoccupied with my problems, my anxieties, my worries, extended family issues.

But in comparison to so many others, near and far away, *"My problems were at zero." Absolutely no comparisons!*

That may be a helpful thought to control our minds, to bring our minds back to a sense of being thankful, humble, and positive.

> For God hath not given us the spirit of fear;
> but of power; and of love and of a sound mind.
> (2 Timothy 1:7 KJV)

Jesus said:

> In the world ye shall have tribulation but be
> of good cheer; I have overcome the world. (John
> 16:33 KJV)

Realize Your Own
Spiritual Need First!

⤶⤶

I don't recall where or when I first heard an old spiritual song that went something like this, "Not my brother, not my sister, but it's me, Oh, Lord, standing in the need of prayer."

So often, even as Christians, we are prone to think that looking out for ourselves is an arrogant, prideful thought.

Yet, so often, as we look at the Scripture, we see the importance of caring for and daily concern for our own spiritual well-being.

The thief on the cross, dying beside Jesus said, "Lord, remember *me* when thou commest into thy kingdom" (Luke 23:42 KJV).

The King of Israel, David, chosen by God, spoke of himself repeatedly in Psalm 23.

So, *"Not my brother, not my sister, but it's me, Oh, Lord, standing in the need of prayer." That's not a selfish prayer. Just urgently needed. Daily.*

The Lord is my shepherd I shall not want.
(Psalm 23:1 KJV)

I can do all things through Christ which strengthened me. (Philippians 4:13 KJV)

Hopefully Have Two Great Gifts

ꙅꙮꙅꙮ

Someone said that *"a Bible that is falling apart belongs to a person who isn't."*

I've previously informed you that my parents were not well-off when I was growing up. When I left home to go away for college, I was hitchhiking. I did not own a car.

But two main things my parents were able to give me on Christmas, December 25 of 1949, were a Bible and their blessings.

On the inside cover page of my Christmas gift that year, a Bible, were these words:

> *May God always bless and keep you.*
> *From Mother and Dad*
> *Dec. 25, 1949.*

I was fourteen years old. After getting the Bible, I was glad to have it.

But as I look back over the years, I have also been glad to receive and cling to their blessing. It's a great gift greater than money to have the blessing of God-fearing parents. The Bible and their blessing—together, they have kept me together. *And at times help put me back together.*

That Bible dated December 25, 1949, is falling apart from wear and tear. Several others are also very well-worn.

> Wherewithal shall a young man cleanse his way by taking heed thereto according to Thy Word. (Psalm 119:9 KJV)

> Thy Word is a lamp unto my feet, and a light unto my path. (Psalm 119:105 KJV)

Receive and Read the Bible

༄༅

As I was handing him a copy of the New Testament and Psalms and Proverbs in a Contemporary English Version, he readily reached toward me, obviously very willing to accept the gift.

Earlier in conversation with him and another peer employee, he informed me that while I had given one to his fellow employee, I had not given him one.

So eager for him to receive one of the CEV New Testaments, I immediately rushed home, secured one of the New Testaments, and brought it back to him.

As he received it, he smiled and said a few words that indicated his gratitude and positive attitude.

The main thought that came to me was his gracious openness and receptivity to my giving him a copy of God's Word to read.

No rejection. No negative spirit. No close-mindedness evident.

Thought. We all have the God-given ability to accept or reject His Word. And we must read it to get it into our minds and hearts.

> *Blessed is he that readeth and they that hear the words* of this prophecy, and keep those things which are written therein: for the time is at hand. (Revelation 1:3 KJV)

> So then faith cometh by hearing, and hearing by the Word of God. (Romans 10:17 KJV)

Seek God First, the Exactly Follows

❧❦❧

I t was exactly what I wanted at the moment. She had asked me what I wanted for breakfast earlier. The question had somewhat more intensity in it because I was sick with flu-like symptoms. Arms aching. Not feeling well. Some weakness. Low fever of 101. Lying around most of the time on the bed.

So when she served me grits and eggs for breakfast, that is grits and eggs mixed together in a bowl, I immediately thought, *That's exactly what I want.* Now, only a true Southerner would appreciate and understand what I mean. Exactly, means not just sort of but numerically like two and two is four. Three and three are six. It was exactly what I had a taste and desire for. Grits and eggs.

The truth of the matter is that Gayle, my wife, has been and knows what I've needed for sixty-four years. Since the day I first laid eyes on her, she was only seventeen, I knew. She was exactly what I wanted and needed for a wife. She has been and still is my friend, counselor, loyal supporter. Been with me, climbing the hills and walking through the valleys of life. But always the strong person that she is. She is a tough marine but at the same time a beautiful lady. Next to having accepted Christ as my Savior by faith, I know she is God's greatest gift to me. Exactly!

> But seek ye first the Kingdom of God, and
> His righteousness; and all these things shall be
> added unto you. (Matthew 6:33 KJV)

Be Thankful for Ordinary and Special Days with Your Spouse

⤞⧜⧜⤝

As I write this, today is December 7, 2020. It was on this day on a Sunday morning, 1941, that the Japanese declared war on the United States. I was six years old. That day began World War II, for the US FDR was president. It was a "day of infamy," he said. Shortly afterward, the United States declared war on Japan. Later, someone said that Japan had "awakened a sleeping giant" to their dismay and later destruction.

That was then, so long ago. This is now. I am now eighty-five. Seventy-nine years later. Today, for me, is not infamous. It's ordinary in a way but also very special. I'm still alive. Gayle, my wonderful wife, is still with me, since June 5, 1957. So that fact alone lifts this day from infamous or ordinary to special.

Earlier, I was thinking that if every man could have a wife for sixty-plus years, as I have, that would surely be a powerful factor in his being wise and successful. She is and has been all these years, since she was twenty, the example of the woman described in Proverbs 31. In addition to that, she is beautiful, still at eighty-three years of age.

I'm thankful to God and to her.

> This is the day which the Lord hath made;
> we will rejoice and be glad in it. (Psalm 118:24
> KJV)

Understand Marriage Is Wonderful, Yet Complicated

⁓◉⊙⊙◉⁓

"We should not have gotten married." That is what she said. The surprising, almost-shocking statement was made by a married woman who had been married more than fifty years. She has grown children and has several grandchildren. She and her husband, likely since their teens, have been devoted Christians and active church members.

Why or how could a married woman say that after so many years of a seemingly successful marriage?

They seemed, from outward observation, like a perfectly matched couple, but were they?

Both were firstborn children. That may have been a problem because, often firstborn, both want to be in charge. No army needs two generals leading the same group of soldiers.

That being said, the truth of the matter is, marriage is extremely complicated and problematic. The expectations both from husband and wife are so high. Often, they expect that *in love* feeling to last forever. It does not. Only two years at best. There may be those rare exceptions. Rare!

Actually, it takes a lot of work for both people to stay together. There are no such things as perfect matches. Usually, it is a puzzle with pieces of the puzzle missing, never to be found, even by this couple mentioned.

Reading the Bible daily and thinking about it help people to keep on loving one another even though they may not feel *in love*. They still do love one another in spite of missing pieces to a puzzling relationship. *Thus, imperfect people are enabled to live together in an imperfect marriage with their imperfect selves.*

> For this cause shall a man leave his father and mother and shall be joined unto his wife, and they two shall be one flesh. This is a great mystery. (Ephesians 5:31–32 KJV)

Be a Good Friend

ఴఠ౬౬ల

Amy was playing with her two older sisters. At the time, she was only three or four years old. One sister was five years older. The oldest was nine years older. They were spending time together casually, innocently, with a game that had rules. Suddenly, one of the older girls took advantage of the youngest. The youngest responded with, *"You not being a good friend."* No loud voice, just a calm, conversational tone. "You not being a good friend" to her older sister. All three are our grandchildren.

Lesson point: Our words and actions can often be so powerful. They can be corrective. Demeaning. Unfriendly. Hurtful. *Or* they can be very friendly and encouraging.

Every day, we have the opportunity to be good friends or not be good friends. You may have no idea how much the person near you needs a good friend. An encouraging word!

Consider the person or persons you work with. *Consider your own family. Every day, everyone needs a good friend. Young and old!*

> Behold, thou hast instructed many, and thou hast strengthened the weak hands. (Job 4:3 KJV)

> A man that hath friends must show himself friendly: and there is a friend that sticketh closer than a brother. (Proverbs 18:24 KJV)

Realize a Broken Life Can Be Fixed

A few months ago, I was driving down Fury's Ferry Road when the engine suddenly, without any warning, cut off.

Stopped running.

The diagnosis was that the timing belt had broken even though it wasn't time for it to be changed. *"It shouldn't have happened."* All service records validated that conclusion.

Anyway, the engine was rebuilt. Since then, it performs like it did the first day I bought it.

Because it performs so well, I'm very sure that the Master Mechanic rebuilt the engine *exactly according to the directions of the manual.* He didn't halfway or partially go by the book.

Thought. Sometimes, life may break down in spite of our best efforts.

It shouldn't happen, but it does. There is a *book* to go by to fix it and to service it. The Bible. *I encourage you to read it daily, especially Proverbs and Psalm 1.*

> All scripture is given by inspiration of God, and is profitable for doctrine, for reproof, for correction, for instruction in righteousness. (2 Timothy 3:16 KJV)

The What, the How, and the Why

‹‹◦○◦››

There is a strong connection and relationship between the *What?* the *How?* and the *Why?* in the Bible.

Micah, the prophet, states, "*What* doth the Lord require of thee but to do justly, and to love mercy and to walk humbly with thy God" (Micah 6:8 KJV).

Luke, the physician, relates the story of the Philippian jailer who asked, "Sirs, *what* must *I* do to be saved?" And they said, "*Believe* on the Lord Jesus Christ and thou shalt be saved" (Acts 16:30–31 KJV).

Luke relates also to a certain lawyer asking, "*What* shall *I* do to inherit eternal life?" And Jesus replied, "Thou shalt love the Lord thy God with all thy heart, and with all thy soul, and with all thy strength, and with all thy mind; and thy neighbour as thyself" (Luke 10:25, 27 KJV).

Then there is the *how* clearly stated by Paul, the apostle.

> Everything in the Scriptures is God's Word.
> All of it is useful for teaching and helping people
> and for correcting and showing them how to live.
> (2 Timothy 3:16 CEV)

> The Holy Scriptures are able to make you
> wise enough to have faith in Christ Jesus and be
> saved. (2 Timothy 3:15 CEV)

The *why* is always for your own good in this life and life after death.

> Moses stated, "You shall walk in all the ways
> which the Lord your God hath commanded you,
> *that ye may live, and that it may be well with you.*
> (Deuteronomy 5:33 KJV)

You Must Want It
and Seek It

⤷◉◉◉↲

O ne study I heard of said that most people get what they really want. While we all may question the truth of that conclusion, there is some truth in it.

Regarding wisdom, there must be an "I want it" factor! Wisdom and common sense and healthy understanding are not thrust upon a person, whether they want it or not.

There must be a sincere, "I really desire," "search for," and "seek wisdom." *God will not force wisdom upon you!*

Jesus said, "Seek and ye shall find" (Luke 11:9 KJV). There is definitely a need on our part to want and seek wisdom as long as we live. No one, not even God, will knock your door down. The final question is, *"Do you want wisdom?"* If so, you must seek it diligently! In your heart and mind, you must decide, "I want wisdom! I need it! I will seek it!" And the beneficiary of that decision and effort will be *you!* Also, one thing for certain, *if you seek stupidity and foolishness, you will find it*; there is so much of it all around!

> Search for wisdom as you would search for silver or hidden treasure. Then you will understand what it means to respect and to know the Lord God. (Proverbs 2:4–5 CEV)

Respond to Insults Like It Never Even Happened

꿍꿍

There is a cleanup business that has a motto or claim that advertises that they make (the mess) look "like it never happened." Fire. Flood. Whatever. They proclaim that they make it look *"like it never even happened."*

That's a strong statement regarding homes and commercial buildings, yards, and landscapes.

However, human relationships, when they get messed up, by strife and conflict, may be more difficult to clean up, but it's possible! How? You might ask. The answer is *simple* but *difficult.*

Recently I observed my wife do it with family members. She ignored an insult and kept quiet. No revenge. Just quietly ignoring an insult toward her "like it never even happened." I felt certain that the family members involved were mentally questioning the situation. Nevertheless, my wife quietly and completely ignored the insult.

Lesson: It takes a great deal of love and wisdom to ignore an insult. However, it takes a lot more emotional and even physical energy to respond and get even. It's best for your own physical health and mental well-being to ignore and keep quiet. Let God handle any needed revenge.

> Losing your temper causes a lot of trouble, but *staying calm settles arguments.* (Proverbs 15:18 CEV)

> You will keep your friends if you forgive them. (Proverbs 17:9 CEV)

Love People—Forgive People

❧

S he said, *"I forgive you, Nanny."* Then after a pause, she added, *"I love you."*

Nanny responded, *"I love you too."*

What had happened a few days before was that Nanny had said something that hurt the grandchild's feelings.

Grant you, her Nanny never intended to hurt her feelings, but the words just popped out, perhaps having not thought through every aspect of the statement. Something we all have done more times than we'd like to admit.

So learning of the hurt feelings, Nanny had called the grandchild and apologized. Thus, came the grandchild's response. "I forgive you. I love you, Nanny."

Thought. In order to maintain relationships with friends, relatives, and everyone else, there must be a lot of forgiveness. Lots of love.

It's not easy. Not always easy to apologize. Not always easy to forgive. The reason people say, "I'm sorry and apologize," is that they love people. The reason people accept apologies is that they love people.

The reason people don't apologize and don't forgive is the lack of love. In the case of this, Nanny, my wife, and this grandchild, there is a great deal of God-given love on both sides of the relationship.

> Love is kind and patient... It doesn't keep
> record of wrongs that others do. (1 Corinthians
> 13:4, 5 CEV)

You, We, Need Intensity

ntensity. It's a factor in life that you need now and will need in the indefinite future.

This morning, I opened a new razor from its package in a box. It was one of those Gillette shaving razors that have five blades, not one, but five! The quickly noticeable thing I experienced was how extrasharp they were. They were definitely different from the previous razors I've been using. Much, much sharper. They glided across my face, as opposed to other razors that pulled at and had difficulty cutting.

The point to be taken here is that in order *to be wise and successful in life, all its issues and happenings, you and I need intensity!*

What is intensity? It's the difference between very sharp and dull. Intensity is the arrow with a razor-sharp point. It's the knife that cuts through tough, hard stuff like it was butter.

In life issues, like work. Marriage. Living a good life. A Christian life. Being an example to others, your kids. Being a parent. A wife. A husband. Yes, we need intensity! Not ordinary! Not dull! Not half-hearted!

We gain intensity in ourselves by daily reading the Bible, especially Proverbs.

> For the Word of God is living and active, sharper than any two-edged sword, piercing to the division of soul and spirit, of joints and marrow, and discerning the thoughts and intentions of the heart. (Hebrews 4:12 RSV)

Be Careful Where and How You Walk and Whom You Walk With

◦◦◦◦◦

My brother, Larry, and I were known to do mischievous things when we were in our teen years.

We went to church, mind you, during those years, but we still seemed to thrive on mischievousness.

Once, when Abbeville leaders decided to add paved sidewalks on both sides of the main street in Abbeville, we observed closely and decided to leave our footprints on the still-wet concrete. We both walked slowly and casually on one whole block of it. We thought we were leaving our footprints for future generations. It was our disappointment when the workers came back and redid the sidewalks. Our footprints are gone.

Thought. The truth of the matter is we all will leave footprints on history. Our families, our friends, and many of our acquaintances will see and feel the influences and consequences of *where* we chose to walk. *How* we chose to walk. And *who* we chose to walk with.

The footprints we make will not be easily erased!

> What doth the Lord require of thee but to do justly and to love mercy, and to walk humbly with thy God. (Micah 6:8 KJV)

> He that walketh with wise men shall be wise; but a companion of fools shall be destroyed. (Proverbs 13:20 KJV)

You Must Seek Wisdom

❧♨❧

Knowledge without wisdom is often dangerous. Position and power without wisdom are dangerous. These three together, knowledge, position, and power, without wisdom are extremely dangerous and destructive.

Destructive to an individual.

Destructive to a family.

Destructive to a society, a nation.

I have seen this and heard this many times as a psychotherapist, personally listening to individuals and family members telling their stories.

Highly educated people, occupying high positions in our society, rich people, who were without wisdom, I've heard their stories. They are destructive to themselves, to their families, *and to our society!*

Wisdom is absolutely necessary for your own well-being! Money. Knowledge. Position. Power. Without wisdom, these will be destructive!

> I am wisdom-common sense is my closet friend… By finding me, you find life… But if you don't find me, you hurt only yourself. (Proverbs 8:12, 35, 36 CEV)

> Respect and obey the Lord! This is the beginning of wisdom. Only a fool rejects wisdom and good advice. (Proverbs 1:7 CEV)

> Proverbs will teach you wisdom and self-control. (Proverbs 1:2 CEV)

Take Care of Yourself

O ne of the last times that Gayle and I flew on a plane was in the 1990s to the Hawaii Island Kauai. We flew from Augusta to Atlanta, then to the West Coast, then to the largest of the Hawaii Islands, then North to Kauai. To make a large understatement would be to say, "It was a long flight."

An interesting statement as they always say by one of the stewardesses just before taking off was something like, "If the plane suddenly loses altitude, an oxygen mask will drop from the ceiling. If you are a mother holding a small infant child, *first* put the mask over *your* face."

Why? Why mother before the child? Easy answer, but an answer in life often not obeyed, not adhered to. Unless the mother is alive, awake, she can't take care of the child.

Unless we take care of ourselves first, *we can't help others.* Taking care of myself spiritually, emotionally, and physically is my responsibility. As much as I possibly can!

Such is not haughtiness. It's a humble God-given responsibility! For me to take responsibility for my spiritual life. My emotional life. And my physical life. As much as possible.

It's okay to *be kind to yourself.* To take care of you! So that you can fulfill your God-given purpose!

David said, "The Lord is my Shepherd; I shall not want" (Psalm 23:1).

Jesus said, "Thou shalt love thy neighbour as thyself" (Matthew 22:39).

Read all of Psalm 23. How many times does David refer to himself? Think about it!

Repeat Great Truths
to Yourself Daily

❧❧❧❧

When I was a kid, before my teen years, in the early 1940s, every Sunday morning during the Sunday school assembly time at church in Abbeville, we would sing, *"Into my heart, into my heart, come into my heart, Lord Jesus. Come in today, come in to stay, come into my heart, Lord Jesus."*

When I say we sang it every Sunday, I do mean every Sunday! It was part of the regular schedule before we separated from the assembly and went to our different age group classes for Bible study.

We didn't need hymn books, and we didn't need a written schedule to follow. We just knew week by week that chorus was to be sung. The repetition got into my mind. Now, it's still in my mind over seventy years later!

There are some powerful truths needed to be remembered in that simple but very biblical chorus. Invitation for Jesus to *come* into your heart. Invitation for Him to *come in today.* An invitation to *stay.*

Jesus wants to be our Savior and the Lord of our lives. He wants us to invite Him into our hearts, our minds, our lives. He wants us to do that NOW, TODAY! And He wants to STAY in our lives for the rest of our lives!

Jesus said to His disciples:

> Stay joined to Me and I will stay joined to you. Just as a branch cannot produce fruit unless it stays joined to the vine, you cannot produce fruit unless you stay joined to Me. (John 15:1, 4 CEV)

Reading the Bible daily helps us to stay joined to Him!

Believe that with God's Help, You Can

⚬⟋⟋⟍⟍⟍

I came in second in the cross-country race that early morning! He was ahead of me no more than fifteen or twenty feet. Ahead of me by a few seconds in a two-and-one-fourth-mile race! We ran almost side by side for most of the race, but he came in ahead of me those last few seconds.

That event happened my senior year in high school in Abbeville, Georgia, 1952–53. I was seventeen. Our new coach, Ray Helsing, had come to our school from up north. He introduced cross-country racing to us. I was glad because prior to his coming, all we had in sports were basketball and baseball. I was not good at either.

Interesting enough, at the beginning of the cross-country racing season, I was the worst runner on the team. The slowest of eleven team members. I was the eleventh man, but I moved to the number two man. That's where I stayed through the whole year. Our team won fourth place in the state. Raced in Atlanta. That was a great showing for a very small school, as ours, racing against very large schools across the state and in Atlanta!

One or two things cross-country taught me was that so much of whether we win or lose is a mind game! It's whether you, yourself, decide *you want to win* and then believe *you can win.* It also taught me that second place or whatever place is perfectly okay if it's the best you can do! Sonny Collins, who ran like a rabbit, was the best runner.

It's important in life to *want to win*, to *believe in yourself* that *you can, and then to give it the best you can.*

I can do all things through Christ which
strengtheneth me. (Philippians 4:13 KJV)

Realize That It's Okay to Be Still and Quiet

cococo

The only way I could find relief from the pain in my wrist, my left arm, and my neck was to stay still with no motion or activity.

The pain was the result of a fall the day before.

Leather-soled shoes, trying to climb an incline, covered with dry pine straw, were recipes for a fall. That's what happened. I fell backward. There I lay groaning, hoping nothing was broken.

So the following day, I felt the soreness and swelling in my wrist.

Staying completely still was the only way I could find relief. No activity. No movement.

When we have been taught to work hard. Stay busy! Don't waste time! Learning to be still is a decision and effort! However, when we have fallen or in pain, physically, emotionally, or spiritually, being still and quiet may be what we really need to find relief and to recover!

> *Be still, and know that I am God...* The Lord of host is with us; the God of Jacob is our refuge. (Psalm 46:10 and 11 KJV)

> For thus saith the Lord God, the Holy One of Israel: in returning and rest shall ye be saved; in quietness and in confidence shall be your strength. (Isaiah 30:15 KJV)

Read the Bible Day or Night

❧❦❧

I t was very early in the morning, before daylight, about five. Mother came into our living room. There I sat. She said something like, "You're up mighty early."

I'm not exactly sure what I said. Just sort of nodded my head. But the fact of the matter was that I had been sitting up all night reading the Bible. I was only fourteen years old. Nothing else was ever said about it.

Looking back, I've often wondered why I was so diligent about reading the Bible that I had received the Christmas of 1949. I had actually told Mother that I didn't want a Bible when she had asked me before Christmas. I was a typical teenager. No drugs. No alcohol. No tobacco. But mischievous!

No one encouraged me to read the Bible. But I would actually sit at night and read five to twenty-five chapters all alone. Why? I don't know! But I do know it influenced me. It affected my thinking and my behavior. Young and teachable.

"The earlier one reads the Bible, the better," is a great understatement!

> And that from a child thou hast known the
> Holy Scriptures, which are able to make thee wise
> unto salvation through faith which is in Christ
> Jesus. (2 Timothy 3:15 KJV)

> Thy word is a lamp unto my feet, and a
> light unto my path. (Psalm 119:105 KJV)

By Being Able to Accept and Go On

੭৩৩৩৩৩

I t had been a beautiful day, sunshine and breeze, on the Chesapeake Bay. But there I was with a Maryland State trooper standing at my side. I, a Baptist minister, was at a row house, one of those narrow two- or three-storied multihousing units in inner-city Baltimore.

Seated in front of us was an older lady. It was my first time meeting her.

Then I said, "We are here to tell you that your daughter fell overboard while sailing with her boyfriend this afternoon in the bay and drowned."

Her daughter was a beautiful, stunningly attractive twenty-six-year-old girl.

The mother did not break into tears. In fact, she hardly moved. Almost like a statue. Still. Stoic facial expression. Seated. She whispered, "Must have been God's will."

But I could feel her grief! In her eyes. In her silence. In her stoic look. I knelt now before her and said a few words and then left with the trooper.

How anyone can accept such loss and go on is amazing! But the truth is that none of our lives can be totally planned or totally protected. Life often demands such of many. Whether God's will or not. Don't know! Life just happens! Loss happens!

> These things I have spoken unto you, that in Me ye might have peace. In the world ye shall have tribulation: but be of good cheer; I have overcome the world. (John 16:33 KJV)

I had fainted, unless I had believed to see
the goodness of the Lord in the land of the living.
(Psalm 27:13 KJV)

Be Friendly with People—
You May Need Them

❧◈◈❧

It was a late Saturday night around eleven-thirty. My brother, Larry, and I were already asleep in our bedroom when our dad came into our bedroom and awakened us. His very strong, demanding words were "Boys! Mr. Sapp is up at his grocery store with the police! He is all upset, scared to death! Somebody wrote on his sidewalk this morning, in front of his house, *'I will kill you tonight at 12:00.'* Do you know anything about that?"

Very sleepy-eyed and half awake, Larry confessed, *"Yes, sir. I did it!"* Larry, at that time, was about fourteen. I was fifteen.

Anyway, Dad said, *"Get up, get dressed! I don't know what he's going to do to you."*

Larry slowly, still half asleep, got up. Dad took him up to Mr. Sapp's store and presented him to Mr. Sapp and the police.

Results were that Mr. Sapp grabbed Larry and hugged him. He was so relieved that it was all a boyish prank with no intent of harm. He pressed no charges. Dad and Larry returned home. Nothing was ever said about it again.

Larry had actually written, with chalk, on Mr. Sapp's sidewalk early that morning before daylight while we were delivering daily newspapers.

I've often wondered why Dad thought one of us did it! Our reputation as teens, I guess. Never asked.

Living in a small town where everyone knew one another, in the late 1940s and early 1950s, had its advantages. Also, Dad had been a customer and friend of Mr. Sapp for years.

> And be ye kind one to another, tender hearted, forgiving one another, even as God for Christ's sake hath forgiven you. (Ephesians 4:32 KJV)

Learn to Live with Yourself

O ne of the most helpful books I've ever read, in fact, studied, is *How to Live with Yourself* by Robert Hastings. The first chapter begins with a fictitious story of a man rushing into a travel agency wanting to schedule a trip anywhere so that he can get away from himself. He is then informed that there are many places to visit but nowhere for him to get away from himself.

The fact is, anyone may ignore others and get away from them. Get away from places. Maybe even ignore a relationship with God. However, the one person we must live with day in, day out, twenty-four seven, is ourselves.

Learning to do that is critical! We all have possible, very personal enemies like self-doubt, fear, anger, anxiety, depression, guilt, and maybe more.

Learning to live with yourself is an extremely powerful motivation and reason to read the Bible daily. It helps you, us, with likely the most critical and important issue, possible problem, we all face! There is no way to get away from yourself! Read Psalm 1 again and especially Proverbs.

> He that hath no rule over his own spirit is
> like a city that is broken down and without walls.
> (Proverbs 25:28 KJV)

The apostle Paul said:

> I keep my body under control and make it
> my slave, so I won't lose out after telling the good
> news to others. (1 Corinthians 9:27 CEV)

Realize Walking
Carefully Is Better

᳗᳗᳗

I was running out to our mailbox in front of our house to pick up
our mail when my feet flew out from under me. Really! My feet
went up higher than my head. I fell flat on my back. There I lay,
groaning, realizing you can't run on ice, especially with leather-soled
shoes.

The year was 1963. We were living out in the country, a few
miles from town, near Carlisle, Pennsylvania. Growing up in South
Georgia, having lived in Pennsylvania for less than a year, I still had
a lot to learn about ice and snow! Real winters! Blizzards! Being
"snowed in" for days! Several feet deep snowdrifts!

After several groans, I picked myself up in my driveway, never
again to run on ice and snow. *Walking slowly* and *carefully* was just
fine! Good enough and a lot safer. It was a painful lesson, but I
learned quickly.

Reading the Bible daily teaches us that *walking is often better
than running! When going through life!* Making a decision! Or just
going to the next thing day by day!

> He hath showed thee, O man, what is good;
> and what doth the Lord require of thee, but to do
> justly and to love mercy and to *walk humbly with
> thy God*. (Micah 6:8 KJV)

Keep Seeking Knowledge
and Wisdom

ꭤꙅꙆꙅꭤ

S he asked me, "Warren, how are you doing?" She was my professor. I was her student at the University of Georgia. The year was
1988. I was fifty-three years of age. The oldest student in my class.
She was probably my age or likely younger.

My response to her caring question was, "I feel like I'm on
vacation!"

She smiled, seemingly to know that I was sharing my hon-
est-to-goodness feelings. Being back in graduate school, for the third
time, away from the work-a-day world's daily stress, was truly like a
breath of fresh air.

Other students were complaining, crying, so to speak, about
the demands of school assignments. To me, I felt like Uncle Remus's
rabbit in the briar patch.

I had been previously in New Orleans once and another time in
Philadelphia in graduate school. This was my first time at UGA. And
I was more than glad to be there. Although several professors seemed
so young, younger than me, I was pleased to be the pupil. Listening!
Learning! None of us ever knows it all!

> If you have good sense, instruction will help
> you to have even better sense. And if you live
> right, education will help you to know ever more.
> (Proverbs 9:9 CEV)

> If you stop learning, you will forget what
> you already know. (Proverbs 19:27 CEV)

Be Careful What Ruts
You Make or Get Into

୧ඉඉ୬

In the car, we were riding down the dirt road on our way to the church in the country, several miles from the town where we lived. Mom and Dad and four children.

The time was the late 1940s. Dad had started, in fact, helped to rebuild a church in a community called Cannonville. The road between our home in town and the location of the newly built small country church was all dirt. No pavement. So when it rained, as it had that Sunday morning, the road was very soft, slippery, clay. Consequently, deep ruts had developed where the cars had made tracks.

Once the wheels of the car settled into the deep familiar ruts, it was next to impossible to get out of the ruts.

Early in life, we all begin to make tracks that soon become familiar and ruts. The ruts of belief, attitudes, and behavior. It's more difficult to get out of our ruts the older we get! *It's extremely important to choose good ruts early in life!*

> Remember, now thy Creator in the days of thy youth, while the evil days come not, nor the years draw nigh, when thou shalt say, I have no pleasure in them. (Ecclesiastes 12:1 KJV)

> Let no man despise thy youth; but be thou an example of the believers, in word, in conversation, in charity, in spirit, in faith, in purity. (1 Timothy 4:12 KJV)

Anticipate the Positive

❧

There I was, in 1944, at the age of nine, picking cotton on my grandfather's farm. At the end of the cotton row was a quart-size mason jar, filled with cool water. Not cold, not hot, just cool. It stayed cool because it lay nestled in the branch under the trees.

You may or may not know what a branch is. It contains some water. Mind you, not an ocean, not a river, not even a large creek. The water may be slightly moving. The main thing is that a branch has trees, sheltering it from the hot sun. It's a quiet, cool, shady place. Nice place to store a quart of water when you have no access to refrigeration.

So when you got to the end of your long cotton row, sweaty, tired, and very thirsty, the cool water in the shady place was very refreshing! It was a great break time! Rest time!

Admittedly, as a young person, nine years old, picking cotton in the hot South Georgia sun, I would eagerly anticipate that cool water awaiting me. Better than a Coke or Pepsi.

Anticipation is a great and wonderful thing when it's positively good! That kind of anticipation enables you and encourages you to endure the long rows and hot sun of life.

> Therefore "Let us not be weary in well-doing: for in due season we shall reap, if we faint not." (Galatians 6:9 KJV)

> The Lord is my Shepherd I shall not want. He maketh me to lie down in green pasture: He leadeth me beside the still waters. (Psalm 23:1–2 KJV)

Realize There Is Blessing
in Some Ignorance

∽◟◟◔◞◞

I was only no more than six years old when he gave me a drink. He called it sweetened toddy. A little bit of whiskey. Lots of tap water. Little sugar.

He was my grandfather Wells, my mother's father, and my middle name is also Wells. So we had some things in common. He was born in 1885. I was born in 1935. Fifty years apart. Yet related. Grandfather. Grandson.

I'm not sure. I don't remember if I was sick with a cold, or what was the reason for my receiving a drink of sweetened toddy. All I can remember is that it was mainly sweet and tart. No, it didn't make me drunk!

I was visiting my grandfather Wells in Daisy, Georgia, near Claxton when this memorable event happened. Memorable because at home with Mom and Dad, growing up, there was no alcohol. None. No beer. No wine. No whiskey. So I never really became acquainted with the stuff. Never acquired a taste for it. Never had any curiosity to check it out as a teenager. *Actually, I consider it ignorance of mine that I'm pleased. Never drunk. Don't know how it feels.*

I say this, write this, mainly for young people. *There are some things you don't need to know to live a great and wonderful life.* You don't have to experience some things! *Sometimes, it's great to be able to say, "I don't know."*

Reading the Bible daily *helps you to know when to say "NO" to* yourself and/or to others. *Read Psalm 1 often and Proverbs daily!*

> Daniel resolved that he would not defile himself with the king's rich food, or with the wine which he drank...and God gave Daniel favor and compassion. (Daniel 1:8–9 RSV)

Realize the War Is Not Over between Good and Evil

❧

Vernon Brown fought in World War II. I knew him well after he came home from the war. He was a US soldier. He fought and survived one of the worst battles toward the end of the war in Germany as an infantryman, on the ground, against Hitler and the worst of his evil empire. Only a few allied soldiers lived to tell about that battle. So many of them paid the ultimate price. Their lives! They died in a battle against evil. They were willing to die that we may live today in freedom.

World War II is over, and most of those heroes are gone now.

The Pattons. McArthur. Roosevelt. Churchill. Truman and the Vernon Browns.

Yet *the war against evil is not over.* We see it. We feel it. Around the world. In our own country, the United States. And in our homes. Maybe that's the worst place. Our homes.

There is a crying need for God's people to awaken and realize there is still a war going on. Against the church. Against everything and person that's good. Christians! There is a great need for soldiers today! Soldiers for good! For God!

Thou therefore endure hardness, as a good
soldier of Jesus Christ. (2 Timothy 2:3 KJV)

Keep Your Priorities in Order

ᒉᕲᕩᕲᕩᕲᕩᒈ

Years ago, I bought and read this book titled *For Preachers and Other Sinners* by Gerald Kennedy. One of the chapters includes the idea of "I didn't go." It's regarding a meeting that the preacher responded with, "I didn't go." Instead, he had decided to stay home with his family that particular evening.

What we read definitely influences our thinking and behavior. So there I was playing basketball at a community court with both of my sons, Alan and Wayne, ages about twelve and eleven respectively. After playing with them a while, being tired out, I was lying on the grass beside the court, watching them, thinking, *I'm glad I decided not to go to that meeting. This time spent with them was the best.*

It's so important to read good books that influence us. And it's important to have *our priorities in order, using our limited time wisely.*

Reading the Bible daily definitely helps us to know best how to think, behave and use our time wisely, especially Proverbs and Psalm 1.

> Blessed is he that readeth and they that hear the words of this prophecy, and keep those things which are written therein: for the time is at hand. (Revelation 1:3 KJV)

> These are evil times, so make every minute count. (Ephesians 5:16 CEV)

> Remember, life is short! (Psalm 89:47 CEV)

> Till I come, give attendance to reading, to exhortation, to doctrine. (1 Timothy 4:13 KJV)

Honor God by Asking
for His Help

෬ා෬ා

I t was one of those just regular, ordinary mornings when I was sitting, casually reading the Bible and one of my several devotional
books. Yet I discovered a verse that I had never really seen before that
is with my mind and heart.

The verse I saw, really saw, was found in *Psalm 50:15*. It says
that when we're in trouble and ask God for help, that honors God.
It honors God for us to ask Him for help! That's very interesting to me.
Actually, I had never thought of it that way. *God likes for us to call
upon Him for help! Our cry to Him honors Him! Even when we are in
trouble!*

So I don't need to apologize as someone did to me recently. He
said, "I hate to ask you, but could you—"
Our relationship with God is so totally different.

> Pray to me in time of trouble, I will rescue
> you, and you will honor Me. (Psalm 50:15 CEV)

Be Honest

This happened when I was still in college at Mercer University. I was about twenty or twenty-one.

I had a job working in a grocery store in Eastman. It was in the summertime, the 1950s.

That particular day, I was working in the meat department bagging up, preparing for sale, several packages of ground beef. One pound each. Sixteen ounces per package. I had already weighed the container, the packaging for one pound of beef. It weighed one ounce.

Then the store owner told me to put only fifteen ounces of beef in each container. Mark on each package as one pound of beef.

I verbally disagreed, saying I couldn't and/or wouldn't do that. He was not pleased with me, a very youthful employee. But he didn't fire me. I worked out the whole summer.

It was only one ounce. But still not honest! Very small, short missteps, little wrongs are extremely dangerous because they not only are wrong within themselves but also lead to much bigger ones. A small hole in a dike can eventually cause a break in the dam. A flood!

> If you do the right thing, honesty will be your guide, but if you are crooked, you will be trapped by your own dishonesty. (Proverbs 11:3 CEV)

Be Able to Stand

❦

As I understand history, it was highly questionable whether steel would be strong enough to stand the weight of a train when steel was used to build the first bridge across the Mississippi River.

However, Andrew Carnegie, who was born in 1835, one hundred years before I was born in 1935, believed that steel would be strong enough to bear the weight of a train. So as a believing and risk-taking entrepreneur and industrialist, he had it built, about a mile long, across the Mississippi, linking the East with the West in the United States by rail.

Every person ever born has faced that question in life, throughout life. Will I be able to bear the weight of all that life puts upon me? Sometimes, maybe oftentimes, the weight of life is extremely heavy.

One thing is for sure: We all will be tested! No question about that! And some more so than others!

> God will bless you, if you don't give up when your faith is being tested. He will reward you with a glorious life, just as He rewards everyone who loves Him. (James 1:12 CEV)

Talk to Wise Friends

❦

"She earned it!" Those were the words my longtime, for years, a friend said to me on the phone during a long-distance conversation. I have known Burnis for over fifty years. He's a minister friend originally from Mississippi but served as a Baptist minister in Maryland for most of his adult years until he retired from pastoring First Baptist Church in Frederick, Maryland, where he still lives.

Burnis is now eighty-eight years of age. A widower. Still with a healthy mind! Full of wisdom!

His words, "She earned it!" were referring to Gayle, my wife. We had been discussing my decision in 1982 to return South from Maryland to Georgia.

While I was reluctant to return South, Gayle was very clear and definite in her tearful desire to return to our home state of Georgia.

Gayle had followed me, her husband, for twenty-three years from Georgia to New Orleans; then to Carlisle, Pennsylvania; then to Crisfield, Maryland; then to Baltimore, Maryland; actually Pasadena, Maryland.

So when I voiced to Burnis, my friend, that Gayle wanted to return home to Georgia in 1982, Burnis's response was, "She earned it!" It's often a good thing to discuss whatever is on your mind with a good and wise friend and to realize the blessing of a godly spouse.

> A truly good friend will openly correct you.
> You can trust a friend who corrects you. (Proverbs
> 27:5–6 CEV)

> A man's greatest treasure is his wife. She is a
> gift from the Lord. (Proverbs 18:22 CEV)

Be Grateful

⁓ত⊙ঔ⊷

I t was in the 1940s, likely 1943. I was eight years old, spending the summer working in the fields on my grandfather's farm. He grew corn, peanuts, cotton, and tobacco. We worked Monday through Friday.

But Saturday was a special day. We worked a few hours, but the main event was, it was BATH DAY! We only took a bath once a week even though we worked in the hot sun five days a week! This was South Georgia's 90-degree climate. Sweating plenty!

The interesting thing was there were no indoor bathrooms. No running water. No hot water. There was only a well where cold water was drawn up by a rope and a bucket. The cold water was then poured into a number two washtub outside in the backyard. There, with no shower and no indoor tubs, is where we took our weekly bath with cold water. In the yard! Naked as could be.

Today, I live in a nice suburban home with the nicest of indoor bathrooms. Still bathing, but not in my backyard!

Reading the Bible daily, since I was fourteen years of age, has helped me to remember my past. How it was then and to be grateful for small things today. They really aren't that small, like an indoor bathroom, running water, and hot showers.

> Be thankful and praise the Lord as you enter
> His temple. The Lord is good! His love and faith-
> fulness will last forever. (Psalm 100:4–5 CEV)

See the Good in Your Place

The house I grew up in cost my dad $2,000. It was originally built as a duplex, with two apartments. At first, my parents rented one apartment. Then about 1942, they bought the whole house and converted it into one living space.

It was heated with a large, upright coal-burning stove. No air conditioning. No telephone. Kerosene stove to cook on. Icebox. No refrigerator. No television, of course!

One extremely important fact was the house's location. The front of the house was maybe one hundred feet from a highway. The south side was several hundred feet from a railroad. Shortly to the south also was a bridge over the railroad track. And one mile east was the Ocmulgee River.

So the bridge, the highway, the railroad track, and the river were all vital parts of my growing-up years. Ages six to eighteen. Having a railroad, a bridge, and a river, we never were bored! We found or created fun! It was there for the taking. Great playgrounds!

Also, I fail to mention there was a cow pasture next door between the house and the railroad.

The apostle Paul said:

> I have learned to be satisfied with whatever
> I have. I know what it is to be poor or to have
> plenty. (Philippians 4:11–12 CEV)

Honor Your Father and Mother

⚜

"**B**urnham and sons will give $100!" That's what my father said, OUT LOUD, in a church business meeting in Abbeville, Georgia.

The First Baptist Church was raising money to do some repairing on the building. Folks were volunteering, vocally, out loud, the amount they were willing to give.

My brother, Larry, and I were teenagers, sitting on the back row. Dad's statement was a shock to our ears! We knew without even asking him. Dad did not have $100 to give. We knew our dad hardly had enough money to pay the grocery bill.

So when he added "and sons," we thought that meant money from our paper route. We had already made the money to buy (our) first family car. Really! Not kidding!

However, later, we learned that dad "borrowed" or worked out some way to secure and give the $100 to the church. We really never learned how!

Why $100? Why did he volunteer for $100? The amount of $100 was the top amount anyone donated. Many volunteered to give less than $100. But our dad, though he couldn't really afford it, wasn't going to be the lesser, especially since all the gifts were known by all. In the 1950s, $100 was a lot of money to us.

Nevertheless, my brother and I never questioned our father. Not once! He was the head of the house! In all things! All decisions! We respected his authority. Absolutely!

> Children, obey your parents in the Lord; for this is right. Honor thy father and mother; which is the first commandment with promise; that it may be well with thee, and thou mayest live long in the earth. (Ephesians 6:1–3 KJV)

Learn from God's Amazing Little Creations

         ᘒᓍᕤᕫᕬ

We have a back porch on our house that reaches some twenty feet long and about four feet wide, circular, with steps at the end of it, reaching to the ground.

The interesting thing about our porch at this time of year, springtime, is that two feathered creatures, birds, have decided to make a nest in one end corner, inside a deep, large, empty, five-gallon bucket sitting there upright. There is no top on the bucket, so they have found it easy to access.

It has been enlightening and entertaining for my wife and me watching them for the past couple of months as they carefully and meticulously built their nest one small twig at a time. Like educated architects and trained builders, it has been very clear that they have known well exactly what they were doing. Amazing in fact, their goal, their purpose. Their know-how!

Now there are two baby chicks in the nest. And with the same diligence, they bring food, small, petite worms, to their little ones. So much energy and innate knowledge in our small-feathered friends. Amazing to us. Their daily care for their little children! Birds! Created by God!

> Look at the birds of the air: they neither sow nor reap nor gather into barns, and yet your heavenly Father feeds them. Are you not of more value than they? (Matthew 6:26 RSV)

Look for the Beauty Despite Your Circumstances

~~~

It was a very bright and beautiful Sunday morning for me. Like several mornings in May, the weather had been perfect—seventy degrees, so aware of the cool warmth, slight breeze, and springtime surroundings.

Standing in my front yard, I was very much aware, looking up, of the bright blue sky and the soft white fluffy clouds so still in the skies. And the tall, very tall, pine trees and the green-leaf palm trees standing with majestic beauty, proudly decorating the scenery.

For a moment, I realized how blessed I was to have the gift of sight and the ability to stand and feel. To be aware of my environment. The world. My home. Just observing. Standing. Hearing the birds singing, orchestrating the whole eventful moment.

Reading the Bible daily helps us to stand, to look up, to observe, to be aware, and even to feel the beauty surrounding us. In spite of so many screaming and devastating distractions in our world. Regardless of our own personal circumstances.

> This is the day which the Lord hath made; we will rejoice and be glad in it. (Psalm 118:24 KJV)

> Although…yet, I will rejoice in the Lord, I will joy in the God of my salvation. The Lord God is my strength. (Habakkuk 3:17, 19 KJV)

> Hearing and seeing are gifts from the Lord. (Proverbs 20:12 CEV)

Learn to Meditate,
Read Again

❦

After Moses died, as recorded in the first chapter of Joshua, God spoke to Joshua because Joshua was going to be the one to take Moses's place of leadership for the children of Israel.

Can you even imagine the awesomeness of such responsibility! It was likely unbelievable to Joshua himself, like or greater than Harry S. Truman taking leadership after FDR died in 1945, in my lifetime. World War II was still going on. Roosevelt had almost been like a king for twelve years. Elected president of the United States for four terms.

Anyway, God told Joshua to do only one main thing to guarantee his success, following Moses, filling his shoes, so to speak.

God said:

> This book of the law...thou shall meditate therein day and night, that thou mayest observe to do according to all that is written therein: for then thou shalt make thy way prosperous and then thou shalt have good success. (Joshua 1:8 KJV)

If he would *meditate on God's Word, it would influence him to live right, do right, and therefore be successful.* A powerful truth. Wise guidance. Instruction from God to us still to this day! Wisdom!

Read again Psalm 1 and Joshua chapter 1.

Be Thankful for God's Care from Birth

❦

"**Y**ou were so ugly as a baby that I was ashamed to take you out. Your grandparents would take you out, but not me."

That was the news my ninety-three-year-old mother shared with me three years before she died.

I was her firstborn, the oldest of five children. Mom was twenty-two when I was born, in a house, not a hospital, in 1935. Right in the middle of the Great Depression in rural Georgia.

I've wondered, at times, why there were almost no pictures of me as a child. Actually, only a couple, but there were several of my brother, Larry, born just eighteen months later, after my birth. He was cute.

Not me!

Why did Mother tell me? I'm not sure. She really didn't have to tell me. Nevertheless, it was a little too late to hurt my self-esteem. But it did cause me to question if there was any bonding between a mother and child. And why I was so ill as a child. Almost died with diphtheria at eighteen months.

What it did do for me was to make me aware of God's care for me long before I could care for myself.

> You, Lord, brought me safely through birth,
> and You protected me, when I was a baby at my
> mother's breast. From the day I was born, I have
> been in your care, and from the time of my birth,
> You have been my God. (Psalm 22:9–10 CEV)

Be Kind to
Poor People

❦

It was a cold winter night and very windy, sometime in the late 1940s in Abbeville, Georgia. A knock came at our front door. Dad opened the door. There stood a man, likely in his forties or fifties, asking, begging for food. A total stranger!

As I said, it was dark and very cold, likely a January night.

My dad, seeing the man shivering in the winter cold, immediately invited him into our home. No questions asked!

Then he invited the stranger to sit down at our dining room table. At the same time, he's asking my mother to prepare the man some food. She does! Again, not asking any questions. Quietly attending to Dad's request.

After the man had finished eating, Dad offered to give him money to pay for one night in the local motel.

The man refused the offer and just asked if we had some old newspapers to use as cover. He planned to spend the night in an old deserted house that he had seen "down the road."

In today's world, our society may not recommend such an accommodating response. However, it does reveal the kindness and the risk-taking nature, especially of my father, in yesteryears. I was just a kid observing my mom and dad!

> Be sure to welcome strangers into your home. By doing this, some people have welcomed angels as guests, without even knowing it. (Hebrews 13:2 CEV)

Recognize Your Dependency

A while ago, I read this true story of two triathlon contestants who fell out completely exhausted within some several yards, maybe one hundred, maybe a thousand, before reaching the finish line!

So after all their human efforts, months of discipline, training, sweat and likely tears, the swimming, the long-distance running, and the biking had exhausted both of them before they crossed the finish line. They had tried hard. Given it their very best. But that wasn't enough to make it by themselves!

So what happened was, some observers rushed to help them cross the goal line.

That's an example of God's expectations of us. As believers. As Christians. He wants us to deny ourselves. Take up our cross and follow Him. He wants us to be in character like Him. Not easy to do in a world that is totally against us. It's an uphill battle! Against the current all the way!

Therefore, we need God's help! His grace! His mercy! His strength! Our very best efforts aren't enough. We are never self-sufficient. We are dependent on God!

The apostle Paul wrote:

> And He said unto me, My grace is sufficient for thee: for My strength is made perfect in weakness. Most gladly therefore will I rather glory in my infirmities, that the power of Christ may rest upon me. (2 Corinthians 12:9 KJV)

Be Independent and Dependent

I was happy to get the job for $8 a week, working every day after school and all Saturdays at Mr. Tom Sapp's grocery store. In fact, I was so pleased. I worked so diligently from the very beginning as an eleven-year-old that he soon raised me to $12 and fifty cents for the same amount of time. I liked my job and proved it by working beyond his expectations, working without being told or watched. Finding work that needed to be done. Taking the initiative even as a kid. He noticed and paid me more money.

Of course, one of the things I liked most about the job was the pay. I became somewhat independent from my parents. Having my own spending money. Buying my own clothes. It felt good. I also loaned or gave money to my younger brother. In 1946, $12.50 wasn't bad for a kid.

Very early, I learned to work hard, take the initiative, and try to be independent. Humanly speaking! But not from God! Forever dependent on God! It's important to realize both. Our independence and our dependence!

> We don't have the right to claim that we
> have done anything on our own. God gives us
> what it takes to do what we do. (2 Corinthians
> 3:5 CEV)

Remember the Lighter Moments, Laugh

◦◦◦

My wife said that she woke up this particular morning literally laughing about me, her husband. How could something so funny happen that it was the first thing on her mind in the morning and it woke her up?

The incident that her vivid mind was remembering was as the following.

Previously, the day before, I had told her that I had gone into one of our back, extra bedrooms. I glanced at a full-size door mirror, saw myself, and jumped backward, momentarily frightened by the mirrored image of my own self. Thinking that I had seen someone else in the room. She knows that I am a bit jumpy anyway. Easily frightened! She thought that was really funny.

I suppose laughter is better than tears when it has to do with a wife's thoughts of her husband. I'm not implying that she never experienced the tears. Life, marriage, family. The years are altogether a mixture of both. But it is special and wonderful when one can enjoy the lighter moments! It is possible to make it happen!

Reading the Bible daily helps.

A merry heart doeth good like a medicine.
(Proverbs 17:22 KJV)

Realize We Must Walk by Faith

❧◎◉◐↝

It was early in the year 2020, and I was on my way to a doctor's appointment. I thought about turning around and going back home several times because it was raining so hard. With my vision, I was trying to drive and was almost completely blind.

It reminded me of how it was when we lived near Baltimore, Maryland, when trying to drive in a snow blizzard. It was almost impossible to see ahead. But when you are on a four-lane or even six-lane interstate or beltway, you feel compelled to keep on going forward, in spite of the fact that you can't see very far ahead.

The truth of the matter is that life is so much like that. We often can only see a short distance ahead. We can try our very best, plan, and work hard, but a perfectly clear vision of the road ahead is an impossible dream!

Neither is turning around and going back possible. Time. Our time.

Our life is moving forward rapidly. We can't even slow it down.

When the Bible says that we walk by faith, not sight, the truth of the matter is there is no other option! Clear sight of the road ahead is not even possible! That's why we need to realize that *Faith in God* on a daily basis is so extremely important. No human has twenty-twenty vision into his or her next year, month, day, hour, or even next moment!

> For we walk by faith, not by sight. (2 Corinthians 5:7)

> Jesus said, "Blessed are they that have not seen, and yet have believed." (John 20:29 KJV)

Work Hard

The summer of 1951 was extremely hot. Temperatures in the high nineties, at times over one hundred. I had a job at the local sawmill. I was only sixteen. The work was outside. There were men much larger and stronger than me literally falling out in the heat.

One thing I learned about myself was that the heat and the hard manual labor took my appetite away. Not hungry, I only wanted water or any liquid. No food. So I lost weight, not that I needed to.

Another thing I learned was the pay was not that great. Eight hours a day. Five days a week. Paid less than $30 for the whole week, actually $29 and some change. Paid in cash. Given to us in a small brown paper bag. Why in cash? No check? I never knew.

But I only worked there for six weeks. I got a better job working inside. Some men, lots of them, were there for a lifetime. It was a good experience for me.

Whatsoever thy hand findeth to do, do it
with thy might. (Ecclesiastes 9:10 KJV)

Be Careful with Your Anger

❧◉◉☙

O ne of the dangerous things my brother Larry and I did for fun when we were early teens was playing on sawdust piles not far from our home in the late 1940s. Playing outdoors was the only play we knew. No TVs. No video games. No computers. No cell phones. Outdoors only!

So we found gigantic piles of sawdust to climb. No one ever told us they might be burning inside. Heat combustion. Fire beneath us. Possibility of our falling through thinned layers of sawdust into fire. No safe place to play!

Human anger may sometimes be like that. Beneath the surface. Like an undercurrent. There, but not seen! Nevertheless, very real. Some call it passive aggression. In human relationships, it's difficult to deal with. Like unseen fire.

Reading the Bible daily will help us to deal with anger, our own and others, more wisely, especially Psalms 1 and Proverbs.

> Wherefore, my beloved brethren, let every
> man be *swift to hear*, slow to speak, *slow to wrath*.
> (James 1:19 KJV)

God Loves You and Me

S he said, "Nobody wants me!" That's a pitifully sad statement. It denotes a very sad feeling. Was it true? What exactly did she mean? Whom was she referring to? Her parents? A boyfriend or the absence of a boyfriend? I really didn't know entirely what she meant. She is a grown woman.

However, it did remind me of a time in my own life. I was in my teen years. I was questioning if God loved me. I recall clearly, almost like a newly discovered idea and feeling, that God does in fact love me. How or why that thought came bubbling up, like a newfound spring of cool, clear water, in my mind. Not sure. But suddenly, there it was, strongly in my mind. *God loves me!* It was, needless to say, great thought and moment of awareness on my part.

It's extremely important to be aware of God's love. Any one of us, like the young lady, may wonder if anybody wants us at some time or times. But listen, remind yourself. Tell yourself. It's a fact. True. *God wants you!* You are important to Him! Always! The Creator of the universe! Encourage yourself with these words. *God loves me, this I know!* Think about it.

> Nothing in all creation can separate us
> from God's love for us in Christ Jesus our Lord.
> (Romans 8:39 CEV)

Accept Corrective Words

❧

"**I** love you too, Daddy." Probably there are no words that a parent would rather hear from their child—especially a grown child.

Those were her words, even after I had attempted to give her some corrective advice. Some may have called it criticism. Nevertheless, after speaking my words to her regarding her marriage relationship and closing my instructive comments with my, "I love you," to her, she responded with her, "I love you too, Daddy."

Dianne is our second child. Now in her fifties. The mother of three daughters. Married to John for over twenty years. I was simply reminding her of something she already knew that John is a very good man and deserves her respect. She seemed to accept my words.

Words of instructions and corrections are not always easy to accept. Paul Tournier indicated in one of his books that none of us really like criticism. However, if we truly love someone, words of help and correction may be much needed, regardless of our age.

> A sensible person accepts correction.
> (Proverbs 17:10 CEV)

> If you speak kindly, you can teach others.
> (Proverbs 16:21 CEV)

Listen

One of the most interesting and most helpful books that I've ever read is *The Awesome Power of the Listening Ear* by John Drakeford.

In the book, he relates a story about George Washington Carver, the noted scientist. Glenn Clark asked him what was the secret of his success in discovering so many secrets of nature. The scientist replied, "All my life I have risen at four o'clock and gone into the woods and talked with God...when people are still asleep. *I hear God best* and *learn* my plan."

One of the greatest lessons of life is to learn to listen! To listen to God, to others, and even to yourself! Your best self! It's not only a lesson to learn, *but it's also a decision! The willingness to listen!* Some may lose the ability to hear. Some may refuse the willingness to listen.

Reading the Bible teaches us the wisdom of *willingness to listen.*

> Faith cometh by hearing and hearing by the
> Word of God. (Romans 10:17 KJV)

Jesus said:

> My sheep hear my voice and I know them,
> and they follow me. (John 10:27 KJV)

Know that God Feels and Understands Your Sorrow

⊰◌◍◌⊱

It was a graveside scene. The funeral was for a baby boy. The date of his birth was the same as the day of his death. One date for the two events. Birth. Death. February 8, 1994.

There I was near Savannah with my wife, the grandmother of the child, and with Alan, our son, the father of the baby boy, also with Dana, his wife, the mother of the child.

Obviously, I am the child's grandfather. And the one to conduct the funeral. Prior to this moment, all standing around the graveside, everything had been talked about on the phone. The sorrow of death at birth. The funeral plans. Asking me to be there, say a few words at the funeral.

I admit and confess that up to this point, conversations by phone had been sad, but somewhat matter-of-fact. Not a lot of heavy emotions were expressed.

But when I saw that tiny little, very small, petite, white casket there in front of me, suddenly reality set in. That's my son's son! He has a name, *Alan Thomas! My grandson! Emotions swept over me!* I felt the fact. This is death, the beginning and the end all at the same time! I could hardly get one word out. *Tears! Couldn't talk!* Then I could see and feel the sorrow in my son and his wife!

The Bible teaches us that *God is not so slow to feel with us and to be with us when we call out to Him with our hurts and sorrows and losses. Read it daily!*

Jesus understands. (Hebrews 4:15 CEV)

Let us therefore come boldly unto the throne of grace that we may obtain mercy and find grace to help in time of need. (Hebrews 4:16 KJV)

Realize Pets May Be
Great Companions

It was one of the times when I was visiting with my mother. She was in her nineties, living alone. Dad had died several years ago. We were seated at her small kitchen table with just two chairs. No more than three feet separating us.

I said Mom was living alone, but not entirely. There in the kitchen with us were her three dogs. Her constant live-in companions.

As Mom and I conversed casually, very lightly, nothing serious, the dogs obviously wanted to be included. Wanting to be recognized. Nosing their way at us. Evidently wanting to be petted. They were annoying to me. Noticeably! I did not feel the same regard for the dogs that Mom did.

That's when she expressed her annoyance with me, her first-born child, not her pet dogs, her constant reliable companions. "If you don't like my dogs," and a few other words that I forgot. Nevertheless, I immediately realized my pecking order of importance, at least for that moment and visit, was not ahead of her dogs. I was reminded that pets can be tremendous blessings or companions to older persons!

> For better is a neighbor that is near than a brother far away. (Proverb 27:10 KJV)

> Children with good sense accept correction from their parents. (Proverbs 13:1 CEV)

Call for Help!

⊷⊙⊶

"Help! Help! Help!" These were the words crying out late one dark night from the cracks between the front doors of a small movie theater in a small town in South Georgia. The two small boys, about nine and ten years old, had been locked in the theater. All the employees had closed up and gone for the night.

The two young brothers had obviously fallen asleep. Awakened later in the darkness, fumbled their way, almost sightless in the inside of the deserted building, to the front doors.

So there they were knelt down at the front doors, locked in. How long had they been asleep and left alone? They didn't know. But alone, late at night, in black darkness, they were a bit frightened, to say the least.

Those two kids were my brother, Larry, and myself in the small town of Abbeville, Georgia, in the mid-1940s. Finally, the night shift policeman heard our cry and came to our rescue. He unlocked the doors. No words were said. We ran all the way home. When we arrived home, our parents were asleep in bed. Not waiting up for us! They, being awakened by us, telling our story, seemingly had no interest and said, "Just go to bed!"

I'm sure Mom and Dad just entrusted us to the care of the small-town community. But just thinking about it reminds me that whether I fall asleep or my parents fall asleep, *God is never asleep.* He watches over me and hears my call for help when I am in the dark, locked up, unable to get out of whatever the situation!

> My help cometh from the Lord which made
> heaven and earth: He will not suffer thy foot to
> be moved: He that keepeth thee will not slumber.
> (Psalm 121:2–3 KJV)

Read

A few days ago, while talking to our son, Wayne, he gave his phone to his daughter, our granddaughter, Emma, who is eleven years old. She is very articulate and smart with a very broad vocabulary. Taking the lead in our conversation, she began telling me, in fact informing me, of a series of history books that she was reading! The books that she was so excited about and obviously enjoyed reading were about the Western frontier during the last part of the 1800s. About American Indians. Settlers from the East. Conflicts. Covered wagons. Brave pioneers. Texas. California. Colorado. Washington State. The Oregon Trail.

It was clear to me that she felt strongly about what she had been reading. She was, as we say, well-read and then was recommending that I read the same series. Said that I should read them and that I would like them.

The ability to read is a powerful and positive mental tool. And a great gift! The eyes to see. The mind to perceive and understand. Books available, especially the Bible. Someone said, *"Who you will be five years from now depends on the friends you have and the books you read."*

> The Revelation of Jesus Christ, which God gave unto *Him... Blessed is he that readeth,* and they that hear the words this prophecy, and keep those things which are written therein: for the time is at hand. (Revelation 1:1, 3 KJV)

Ask God to Help
You Truly See

⚜

S he said, "It's a romantic place." The person speaking was our twenty-five-year-old granddaughter. She is a college student. Beautiful
young lady with a very happy spirit, very observing eyes. She laughs
easily at herself, as well at others, and seemingly at life itself at times.

The place she observed and described as *romantic* is part of our
backyard. There is a goldfish pond there with nine bright orange
goldfish, most at least six inches in length, and one coy fish. Several
palm trees, like a Florida scene! Frequently with five or six squirrels
feasting on the sunflower seeds or chasing one another. Sometimes
one or two red birds and doves. Also, flowing water over rocks like
a small lively-sounding mountain stream. And beautiful flowers! An
oasis!

So all in all, not hard for Cara, our granddaughter, to see and
describe it as a romantic place.

However, there is something to be said about a person's ability
to see and observe the romance in places. The beauty, the calmness,
the peacefulness! *Reading the Bible daily helps us to see romance and
beauty. In places. In people. And in life!*

> Open thou mine eyes, that I may behold
> wonderous things out of Thy law. (Psalm 119:18
> KJV)

Freely Give Acceptance
and Friendliness

He was a chaplain that worked in one of the major hospitals in Augusta. He was explaining to me that the hospital had a very well-defined policy regarding meeting or seeing people, fellow staff members, or the general public that may be visiting the hospital.

As you met someone in the hallway, you were to speak to the other person. Give them eye contact. All in all, he was saying that you should be pleasant, perhaps give a smile. But *definitely* be friendly. *Accepting* of the other person.

What about that? Sort of like *intentionally being nice to people—cordial.* Give them a very kind demeanor. Smile. Hello. Or how are you? All free of charge. You may not even know the person, or you may never see them again. But how expensive is that? The *gift of acceptance, friendliness, and air of warmth. Would that be a good policy for any place? Person? Church? Home?*

You know the answer to that question! How kind? Cordial? Accepting? Friendly? Are you? Think about it!

> But the fruit of the Spirit is love, joy; peace, long suffering, gentleness, goodness, faith, meekness, temperance: against such there is no law. (Galatians 5:22–23 KJV)

Beware of Sudden Temptation

"Anywhere you want to go." Those were her words when I asked her, "Where do you want me to take you?"

It was a very rainy, late afternoon, as I was driving through downtown Savannah. The sun was about to go down. So with that and the rain, it was not easy to see in the heavy traffic.

Surprisingly, a young woman stepped from the sidewalk, off the curb waving for me to stop, and so I did. She opened the passenger's door, and suddenly, there she was sitting in my car. Then, came the, "Anywhere you want to go," answer to my question. She was not dressed for the part. Just blue jeans and a shirt.

But I quickly realized the situation and said, "I'm sorry, ma'am. I guess I misunderstood." Then I stopped the car and let her out.

In life, stupid situations may suddenly jump out in front of you when you least expect it.

> There hath no temptation taken you but such as is common to man: but God is faithful, who will not suffer you to be tempted above that you are able; but will with the temptation also make a way to escape, that you may be able to bear it. (1 Corinthians 10:13 KJV)

Know that God Understands

There I was, in the hospital in Atlanta. This happened many years ago.

I was hospitalized for my depression. I had just recently moved from Maryland to Georgia. Keep in mind that I grew up in South Georgia. Lived in Georgia until I was twenty-four years old.

Now in Atlanta, twenty-three years later at forty-seven years of age, I was severely depressed. So depressed that I had no memory of the move from Maryland to Georgia.

The reason for my move at forty-seven years of age was a change of job. I decided to leave a job I dearly loved. The main reason was to move back South. In other words, to go back home. Emotionally, I learned that you indeed, *"can't go back home again."*

So there I was literally emotionally broken down in grief. I felt like no one understood. And no one really was able to help me. This was my sadness! My grief! My problem! In life, some things sometimes are like that! Our birth! Our death! Moments!

Since that time, I've found help with this Bible verse:

> We have not an High Priest (Jesus Christ) which cannot be touched with the feeling of our infirmities (our weaknesses) but was in all points tempted like as we are, yet without sin. (Hebrews 4:15 KJV)

That verse reminds me that God understands me, my situation, and my feelings even if I don't really understand myself.

Reading the Bible daily, especially Psalm 23, Psalm 1, and Proverbs, definitely helps us find comfort and strength when we feel all alone with ourselves.

Learn to Be Quiet and Listen

∽⋐⊙⋑∽

O ne of the simple fun things that I enjoy doing is browsing through bookstores. My wife accuses me of stealing if I pick up a book and casually begin reading in the bookstore without first buying it. My explanation is, "Not sure yet that I want the book."

So it was one of those times I discovered a book titled *Quiet* by Susan Cain. She is a graduate of Harvard Law School. Interesting, even amazing to me, to find and read by a lawyer about the power and relevance of learning to be quiet, to listen, not to keep talking. It's often a lost art, that is, the ability to stop the noise. Listen. *Be still. Be quiet.* Turn off the TV, the radio.

Quiet is a wonderful experience! You might hear the wind, the rain, the birds chirping, or a friend sharing his or her heart. Maybe even hear God trying to get through to you.

> For thus saith the Lord God, the Holy One of Israel; in returning and rest shall ye be saved; in quietness and in confidence shall be your strength. (Isaiah 30:15 KJV)

Stay Focused on One Thing at the Time

ⲟⲟⲟ

A while back, I was having a conversation with Amy, our twenty-year-old granddaughter, who is a senior at Augusta University. I was confessing to her my frustration over having so much to do, so many things on my plate to deal with.

She looked at me in her very calm, serious, matter-of-fact facial expression and said, *"Just do one thing at the time."*

Now, I've heard that before, of course, but the fact that she said it and the way she said it took root in my mind. I heard her. Thought about it again. Seriously!

It's such a simple statement, but it's classic truth. It's the foundational basis that all specialists build their lives, their work. One thing!

The most important word in her statement, the most significant, is the word *one*.

Learn to live one day at a time. The day I have on hand, now. Not wasting time regretting any yesterdays. Not being anxious about tomorrow. Staying focused, not scatterbrained, trying to juggle more than God ever intended us to do.

The apostle Paul said:

> This One thing I do, forgetting those things which are behind, and reaching forth unto those things which are before. I press toward the mark for the prize of the high calling of God in Christ Jesus. (Philippians 3:13–14 KJV)

Build Your Life on Rock-Solid Principles

❧◉◈◉❧

The time was 1965. The place was Carlisle, Pennsylvania. Carlisle is a twenty-thousand-population city in South Central Pennsylvania. It's the home of the Army War College where about 40 percent of its graduates become generals. Dickinson College is there. All of this is located in a very clean, cultural, northern environment, only eighteen miles west of Harrisburg, the capital, on the Pennsylvania turnpike.

Nevertheless, we were there in the midst of building the first church building for the young Carlisle Baptist Church. The builders were having a big problem with digging and founding the front east corner of the building exactly where the architect had designed it to be. There was a stone there, unmovable! It was solid, large, and deep in the ground. Refusing to be moved even by heavy equipment.

So consequently, the builders decided to rest the front east corner, the foundation of the building on the rock. Thus, the building's foundation was literally built, setting, on solid rock!

Early in life, when we're just beginning our brief earthly journey, it's important to build our lives on solid principles and truth that will stand unmovable through the storms of life.

Jesus said:

> Everyone then who hears these words of mine and does them will be like a wise man who built his house upon the rock; and the rain fell, and the floods came, and the winds blew and beat upon that house, but it did not fall, because it had been founded on the rock. (Matthew 7:24–25 RSV)

Accept the Challenge of Change

❦

"*Tell them we are not coming!*" Those were the words Gayle, my wife, said to me when Stanley Moore called to inform me that First Baptist Church, Crisfield, Maryland, wanted me to accept the job as their pastor.

So in response to Gayle's statement and also my own feelings of reluctance, I went down to Crisfield, on the Eastern Shore of Maryland. There I sat with their committee to try to convince them that I was not the man for the job.

They convinced me otherwise! So we accepted the job that *I almost refused!* In less than a month, my wife and I and our four children fell in love with the place! We lived there 1967–1972. Five wonderful years!

Crisfield is a small Chesapeake Bay town, right on the water. In 1920, it was considered the Oyster Capital of the World! Later, it was known as the Crab Capital of the World!

In 1967, it was neither, but it had an atmosphere, a spirit, among the people that was indescribable! A love. A warmth. Our whole family felt their acceptance immediately! To this day, over fifty years later, my wife and I speak of Crisfield with love and affection. We almost didn't go there! We're so glad we did!

Reading the Bible daily helps us to gain the strength and wisdom to accept the challenge of change. We may be reluctant to leave our comfort zone. But later, we're so glad we did!

> For we walk by faith, not by sight. (2 Corinthians 5:7 KJV)

Be Careful with Your Eyes

I am often amazed at the power, the influence, of a look from someone else, the glance of their eyes at you. There is the tremendous power of influence without a word being said. It's just the way the other person looks at you and maybe their demeanor that you read as being powerfully positive or negative.

I recall once it happened to me. I was only thirty-two years old. I was in Crisfield, Maryland. 1967. The setting was in a meeting with a committee of five people. They were verbally trying to convince me to accept a job that I was reluctant to do so.

But there was this one older lady that turned her head and looked at me. That was the small but *powerful look* that influenced me to say yes. There was in her eyes a look of encouragement. Need, warmth, and wisdom.

Gayle and I both learned to love the job and the people. That particular woman and her husband became our dearest of friends for years to come, in fact, to their deaths. We shared in the grief and loss at her funeral in Crisfield, Maryland.

Lesson: Never underestimate the way you look at people. Your glance. Your eyes say a lot without a word being spoken. Love or hate! Like or dislike! Positive or negative! *Our eyes mirror our hearts!*

> When He saw the crowds, He had compassion for them, because they were harassed and helpless, like sheep without a Shepherd. (Matthew 9:36 RSV)

Remember to read Psalm 1 and Proverbs.

Stay Aware of Your Weakness

Some years ago, I read this book by Paul Tournier titled *The Strong and the Weak.* He was a Swiss medical doctor, theologian, and author of many books. At one time I had read every book he had written. Anyway, the thesis of the book was that the weak are sometimes strong and the strong are sometimes weak. His admonition was for us not to assume of ourselves or others that we are always weak or always strong.

Such was Apostle Peter, overestimating his strength when he said something like, "Lord, others may deny you but never me." Later, after he had denied Christ three times when Jesus asked him, "Simon Peter, do you love me? Like, I love people. With the same kind of (agape) love?"

Peter wasn't so self-confident. He had learned not to overestimate his own strength.

It was after he became aware of his own weakness that God was able to make him strong! No one has unlimited spiritual strength! We make it in life wisely and successfully as we stay aware of our human weakness, limitations, and dependency on God for strength!

Peter said:

> Be sober, be vigilant; because your adversary, the devil, as a roaring lion, walketh about seeking whom he may devour. (1 Peter 5:8 KJV)

Paul said:

> And He said unto me, My grace is sufficient for thee; for My strength is made perfect in weakness. Most gladly therefore will I rather

glory in my infirmities, that the power of Christ may rest upon me...for when I am weak, then am *I* strong. (2 Corinthians 12:9–10 KJV)

Forgive!

He said, *"I hated him for seven years, but now, the hate is gone!"* The hate ate at my insides for seven years, but now it was gone. *I'm glad you called me because I wanted to tell you, Dad!"* Yes, the man telling me this story was my son Alan.

I knew the situation. The man he forgave had stolen, taken from him in a bad business deal. The amount of $100,000. My son was not rich. It was, in fact, borrowed money that my son really didn't have, so he owed an extra $100,000 that had crippled him financially for years. Hurt his credit rating. It was indeed a dirty deal he accidentally fell into.

So for him to say, *"I've forgiven him. No longer is the hate eating at me."* I was amazed and *proud of him.* The debt was not paid, but he forgave him anyway!

One thing that motivated my son was God, he said. Also, he saw his *debtor at a graveside,* having just tragically *lost his only five-year-old granddaughter.* Alan, being there also at the graveside, seeing the grandfather's grief, went over to *comfort him and hugged the man.* Alan said that as he did that, *his hate went away as the man broke down weeping.*

I told Alan how *proud of him* I was. That it took a *big man* to do that. Alan said again, emphasizing, that his *hate was gone!* He felt so much better. Himself!

Admittedly, forgiving is not easy, but hating *will eat at you internally.*

Forgiveness is best for both parties!

Reading the Bible, *with God's help, you can forgive.*

> And be ye kind one to another, tenderhearted,
> forgiving one another, even as God for Christ's sake
> hath forgiven you. (Ephesians 4:32 KJV)

Know and Believe the Truth

It was in the early 1950s. I was in high school in Abbeville, Georgia. Mr. Dix was one of my teachers. He lived alone between Abbeville and Fitzgerald, out in the country, at a very well-known and large flowing spring of very clear water. Beautiful. Clean. Cold. And clear!

Often people would visit the spring, Mr. Dix said, and they would ask the question, "How deep is the spring?". He would inform them. Then they would frequently say, "I don't believe the water is that deep." Of course, the water was so clear; they were looking through the water.

Nevertheless, his response to their statement of unbelief was, "Your belief has nothing to do with how deep the water is. Whether you believe it or not, still the water is as deep as I'm telling you." They needed to know the water was deep that they were about to swim in. Their life may depend on it!

So true in life. Truth exists. Truth is absolute. The water was, in fact, just as deep as he said. *It's extremely important that we, I, know the truth.* And *believe the truth! Our life does depend on it!*

Reading the Bible daily helps us to accept, believe, and know the truth!

Jesus said:

> I am the Way, the Truth, and the Life; no man cometh unto the Father, but by Me. (John 14:6 KJV)

> For God so loved the world that He gave His only begotten Son, that whosoever Believeth in Him should not perish, but have everlasting life. (John 3:16 KJV)

Endure

❧

She was crying herself to sleep night after night. She had just given birth to Wayne, our second son, our fourth child. She was already home from the hospital, but not our newly born son. September 1966. In Carlisle, Pennsylvania.

He was still in the hospital lingering between life and death. He had two of the best pediatricians available anywhere, but young baby Wayne could not retain food in his stomach. The only way he was being fed was with a needle through a vein in the top of his head. Not a pretty sight. Baby lying there with the needle in his head.

Mother was at home with Father. Mother had gone through the nine months of pregnancy. Then she had the pains of giving birth in her white-knuckled stoic fashion. The baby was left in the hospital. Will he make it or not? Question and tears for twenty-one days.

Well, Wayne did! After a very difficult struggling, questionable start, uphill at the first breath of life, Wayne climbed that hill and now, many years later, married, and became the father of three himself. He endured.

Life! The Christian life! It's more than a birth. Spiritual birth is just the beginning. The apostle Paul spoke of the Christian life as a *race* to be run to the finish line. He spoke of it as being like a *soldier* in a battle. *Not easy! He used the word endure!*

The apostle Paul said to young Timothy:

> Thou therefore, my son, be strong in the grace that is in Christ Jesus. Thou therefore endure hardness, as a good soldier of Jesus Christ." (2 Timothy 2:1, 3 KJV)

Realize You Need Two
Canes to Lean On

ﾟ◌◌◌ﾟ

O ne of my memories of my father, when he was in his late seventies or early eighties, was him standing on his back porch, leaning on his walking cane. He was standing up, but his cane was something he definitely needed.

For some reason, it's a very clear snapshot, a picture, that I can see visualizing in my mind. It's amazing how our minds can store pictures, never to be erased. I can see him alive, speaking, his facial expression, leaning on the cane.

Today, I own that cane, and I use it. I've realized that I can walk with much more confidence, not to fall, with a walking cane.

Truth is, in life, in order to *stand* and *walk* with confidence and assurance, we all need a relationship with God above to lean on. And we need earthly ties with friends, good friends! None of us need ever to try to walk or stand alone! Thus, we all need two canes, regardless of age! *The vertical relationship with God. The horizontal relationship with wise friends.*

Even Jesus said to Peter, James, and John the night before His crucifixion:

> My soul is exceeding sorrowful, even unto death: tarry you here, and watch with me. (Matthew 26:38 KJV)

> And the Lord God said, it is not good that the man should be alone. (Genesis 2:18 KJV)

> God is our refuge and strength, a very present help in trouble. (Psalm 46:1 KJV)

Be Thankful for Your Working Mother—Inside and Outside the Home

୧৬৩୨৬৩୨৩

As a kid watching my mother every Monday, I wondered why did she cook our dirty clothes in a large black iron pot outside in our backyard. That's right; she would build a fire under a black kettle and cook the dirty clothes in boiling water in our backyard.

After that, she may take some of the clothes and scrub them against a rough metal washboard using homemade potash soap.

After all that hard work, she would dash the clothes in clear, cold water. Rinsing the soap out of the clothes three times, from one tub to another, three separate tubs.

Then by hand, she would twist each piece, squeezing the water out of each.

After all that effort, she would gently hang the clothes on a wire clothesline, stretched between two poles to dry in the sun.

Later in the day, before dark, she would gather each piece from the clotheslines and take them in the house. There to be carefully folded or ironed smoothly, all by hand. A full day's work! Once a week!

Those were the days in the 1940s before machine washers and dryers were common. Those were also the days when being the wife of a husband and the mother of five children was a full-time job. No questions asked. Working outside the home and inside the house even back then! Full-time job! Hard work! *So be thankful for your working mother!*

> Honor thy father and thy mother: that thy days may be long upon the land which the Lord thy God giveth thee. (Exodus 20:12 KJV)

> Charm can be deceiving, and beauty fades away, but a woman who honors the Lord deserves to be praised. Show her respect, praise her in public for what she has done. (Proverbs 31:30–31 CEV)

Learn to Walk by Faith, Not Sight

"Why do you have your lights off?" That was the question asked to a blind student by a sighted student. The question was sensible to the sighted person but made no sense to the blind student. He roomed alone in his dorm room. Light of day or darkness of night made no difference to him. Both were the same. He was blind.

This event happened frequently at Norman College, a small junior college in South Georgia that my wife and I attended in the mid-1950s. It was a Christian school, a great place for kids, eighteen years of age, right out of high school, and away from home for the first time.

Nevertheless, back to the blind student. He functioned very well on the small, very calm, and congenial campus. He knew his way around night or day.

Truth is, in a way, we're all blind to tomorrow, next week, month, or year. The future is unknown to us. We can't see into it! We can't predict it! Life is brief, fragile, and uncertain. Unpredictable!

Reading the Bible helps us to gain the *wisdom and faith* to manage the uncertainty of life and our blindness to the future! Although we can't see into the future, we can learn to walk into it with confidence.

> Boast not thyself of tomorrow; for thou knowest not what a day may bring forth. (Proverbs 27:1 KJV)

> We walk by faith not by sight. (2 Corinthians 5:7 KJV)

Trust Your Best Inner Self

Gayle and I were visiting Vancouver, British Columbia, Canada, in the 1990s. While there, of course, we walked around to learn more about the far Northwest.

One particular day, we visited this deep gorge, probably two hundred and fifty feet deep. Really deep! And wide! There was a swinging bridge, held up by ropes, hanging across the gorge. We stood there watching several people daring to trust that narrow, maybe four feet wide, walkway bridge. They walked across. We started to trust it, but after about three steps, we were filled with discomfort and anxiety. We decided not to dare it. Definitely outside our comfort zone!

What about that? Were we cowards? Chickens? No guts to try it? Other people were. Shouldn't we prove something to others or ourselves?

Or was it okay just to say to ourselves, "Not comfortable with that!" Do we have to prove ourselves by doing something just because others are doing it?

Self-acceptance is extremely important! We all have emotional and physical limitations. It's not always wise to break out of your comfort zone! *Your comfort zone may be your character!* It's okay to trust your gut! Your inner self. And walk away from some event or happening. You don't have to prove yourself to others! God made you who you are!

> The devil took Jesus to the holy city and had him stand on the highest part of the temple. The devil said, "If you are God's Son, jump off. The Scriptures say: 'God will give his angels orders about you. They will catch you in their arms and you won't hurt your feet on the stones.'" Jesus

answered, "The Scriptures also say, '*Don't try to test the Lord your God!*'" (Matthew 4:5–7 CEV)

The apostle Paul said:

> I am not trying to please people. I want to please God. (Galatians 1:10 CEV)

> Our inner thoughts are a lamp from the Lord. (Proverbs 20:27)

Reading the Bible, especially Proverbs, teaches you when to walk away! Trusting your gut, your inner self. Accepting yourself! Wisdom!

Realize Boundaries Are
for Our Own Good

This happened a few months after we moved into our current home, in June of 2018 at 602 Saw Grass Drive. We have this pond of goldfish in the backyard. It is about ten by ten feet and maybe three feet deep in the middle. Our daughter, Dianne, had supplied it with about twenty fish.

Anyway, for some reason, every one of those fish either swam or were washed up on the banks of the small pond. Out of the pond, they all died. They were never meant to live outside the boundaries of the pond. They were created to live and breathe in the water, only in the boundaries of the pond.

Theoretically, were the fish thinking, *We don't like the boundaries of this small pond? We want out. No limits. No boundaries. Freedom!*

Humans were also created by God only to survive, to live best, to strive within certain and definite boundaries. *Bursting out of God's set boundaries, we humans don't do well.* We don't even breathe. We, in fact, die! *Like fish out of water!*

The boundaries and guidelines. They are all clearly described in the Bible. Reading the Bible helps us to know the boundaries and stay within the boundaries. *For our own good! Especially Psalm 1 and Proverbs.*

> And the Lord said… O that there were such a heart in them, that they would fear Me, and keep all my commandment always, that it might be well with them and with their children forever! (Deuteronomy 5:28, 9 KJV)

For the wages of sin is death; but the gift of God is eternal life through Jesus Christ our Lord. (Romans 6:23 KJV)

Be Good Parents to Your Children

It was a beautiful sunny afternoon in my backyard. There with me, very close by and easy for me to observe, were my three great-grandchildren. One was four years of age, Brooklyn. Addilyn, her sister, was two. Their cousin, Lucy, was three.

Conflict was happening in the mix among the three of them. Whom would anyone guess to be the dominant one of the three? Not the oldest or even the next to oldest. The two-year-old! Her attitude, her demand, was very clear. She wanted a simple two-feet-tall ordinary-looking small stick. Not colored, not beautiful. Just a small limb, obviously fallen from a tree.

After her wise and gentle mother made her calm down and return the stick to her sister, she reached out *again* and *jerked* the stick away for her own possession.

How could, and why would, a two-year-old be dominant, relating to a four-year-old. The fact of the matter, such behavior is not uncommon for children. God made all of us different. Different personalities. Some gentle and easygoing. Some not. Some outgoing. Some quiet. It's not easy to explain.

Nevertheless, the one thing we all need from early childhood is good parenting. *Bible teaching. At home! Wise is the parent who realizes this! And blessed are the children!*

> And these words, which I command thee this day, shall be in thine heart: and thou shalt teach them diligently unto thy children. (Deuteronomy 6:6–7 KJV)

After the Tears, What?
Accept. Go On!

ෙ❦෨

O ne of the saddest accounts of history in the Bible is that of David, King of Israel, the former shepherd boy. But this particular moment was not one of victory over the giant, Goliath. It was not when in all his glory he was anointed King. It was not when he got the desire of his life, Bathsheba.

It was a time that "he wept." His son Absalom had just been killed. He said, "My son, Absalom! Would God I had died for thee, O Absalom, my son, my son!" (2 Samuel 18:33 KJV).

The acute sadness was that his son had been killed, and his flood of tears could not change the situation. Could not return his son to life. David had to *accept* the death of his son. It was not just death. It was the *death of his son.*

So what does anyone do with loss like the death of your child or loved one?

Even tears! Like a flood! Cannot change the situation! I said to a person who recently asked me that question. "What does a parent or a grandparent do?"

My response was, "It may just rip your heart out!"

So your heart may be ripped out, you may have wept seemingly, a flood of tears. What then? Accepting what you can't change is not easy! But even though with a broken heart, *David did accept it and go on, and you can too.* Like David, *with God's help.*

David may have written Psalm 23 with tears when he said:

> Yea, though I walk through the valley of the shadow of death, I will fear no evil for thou art with me. Thy rod and Thy staff they comfort me! (Psalm 23:4 KJV)

Listen and Follow Directions

❦

There is an extremely important Scripture found in the Gospel of John, chapter 10, verses 27–29.

The Scripture verses describe who are God's sheep. In other words, who are His people? Jesus says that His people *know His voice* just like the sheep of a certain shepherd recognizes the voice of their shepherd.

Then Jesus says that when His people *hear* His voice, they will then *follow* Him. Jesus continues to say that *He knows His people.* He knows His people by name.

What we have here is a very clear definition of the people of God. God's people are listening to Him. And they are following Him. Two very important verbs here describe a person who believes in Jesus Christ. They are *listening to Him* and *following Him.* Both of these present active verbs are evident, visible, and noticeable. They are deliberate. A person has to decide to do both.

Listen. Follow. The listening and the following show that they really do *believe!* The reward of this is eternal life. Absolutely. Jesus says in this same passage of Scripture, "I know this person." "Nothing" or "no one" can take this person from God. This person is *eternally secure* in the loving, caring arms of the Shepherd.

Lesson: Reading the Bible is a way of listening to God. And it encourages and enables us to believe and to follow, especially Psalm 1 and Proverbs.

> My sheep hear My voice, and I know them and they follow Me: And I give unto them eternal life; and they shall never perish, neither shall

any man pluck them out of My hand. (John 10:27–28 KJV)

Listen carefully to My instructions, and you will be wise. (Proverbs 8:33 CEV)

Be Grateful for Good Friends

❧◎◎☙

A school classmate of mine, Carol Culpepper, called me a few days ago from Abbeville to inform me that another one of our classmates, Ernest Harvey, had just died at age eighty-four. He, too, lived and worked near Wilcox County, Georgia.

Ernest went on to become a research scientist. PhD. He developed the peanut that today is used in all Mars candy products, including the famous Snickers bar, my personal favorite candy.

My point in all of this, being reminded of Ernest's death, is the era in which we grew up. Those twelve years we were together in 1941–1953. A small school, less than four hundred pupils in total. Small town, Abbeville, about a thousand people.

A time when drugs were not a problem. Time with no cell phones, no computers, not even televisions. Most of us were relatively poor compared to today's standards. We did not consider ourselves poor.

Because we felt then and still do now as we look back, we had everything! *Everything we needed and more!* We were content, very happy. I never remember ever being bored or unhappy as a teenager. Even though I never had a car of my own until later in college.

A lesson of gratitude as I look back. Thankful that I was blessed to grow up in such a wonderful time with such *great people*. I feel indebted to the time, the place, the culture of less, and especially my *brothers and sisters* in school, like Ernest and Carol and so many others!

> With all my heart I praise the Lord! I will never forget how kind He has been. (Psalm 103:2 CEV)

> Good people are like trees with deep roots. (Proverbs 12:12 CEV)

Accept God's Amazing Grace, by Faith

❧❧❧

It was in 1984. I was pastor of a First Baptist Church in a small southern town in South Georgia. I had a friend, Gene Puckett, whom I had known for several years. In fact, we knew each other when we both lived in Maryland. He was an editor of the Maryland Baptist paper. Then, I knew him when he was working in North Carolina as the editor of the North Carolina Baptist paper.

Anyway, Gene was the one who recommended that I secure and read the book *The Struggle to Be Free* by Wayne Oates. Why he recommended it, I wasn't sure; but having read it and reread it, I know for sure, I needed to read, study, and digest it. I did. And I have recommended it to others many times.

My take from the book, especially for me, is *that I may accept my own limitations. I don't have unlimited energy or strength or even time. Also, I can't nor do I have to try to earn my way into heaven or into God's acceptance.*

It's only by His grace and my faith that I'm accepted by God. I can't earn or buy His acceptance. It's only by His amazing grace and my simple childlike faith. Also, it's often good to be reminded to accept and believe what we say we already believe!

> For by my grace are ye saved through faith; and that not of yourselves: it is the gift of God; not of works, lest any man should boast. (Ephesians 2:8–9 KJV)

Realize Less Is Often Best

⁣⁣⁣⁣⁣⁣⁣⁣⁣⁣⁣⁣⁣⁣⁣⁣⁣⁣

I t's one of those permanent pictures I can still visualize in my mind. It's like others will always be there. I can pull it up on the computer screen of my mind.

It was a typical Saturday. I was walking home for lunch. I knew that my mother had made me my favorite dessert, banana pudding. She would make it for me every Saturday. I was twelve years old, working at Mr. Tom Sapp's grocery store. Making $12.50 a week. It was 1947.

Mr. Sapp's store was very simply arranged and very limited with items if compared to today's massive food stores. But it was a great job for me at twelve years of age. It was simple as life was simple. Plain. Not too much stuff to consider.

It seems *when life is less, not more*, simple, not complicated, smaller, not larger, life has less to be disappointed about! Just to be walking home, from working at a small grocery store, making $12.50 a week, looking forward to Mom's banana pudding was a great day! Enough to smile about! True contentment!

> For godliness with contentment is great gain. For we brought nothing into this world, and it is certain we can carry nothing out. And having food and raiment let us be therewith content. (1 Timothy 6:6–8 KJV)

Reading the Bible daily, especially Psalm 1 and Proverbs, teaches us how to be content!

Enjoy God-Given Moments of Entertainment—the Mouse

⌒⌒⌒

We were on our way to a doctor's appointment in July 2020 when there he was, this little gray mouse, right in the middle of the street. We had stopped for a red light. Then we saw this petite, little creature come running out of the grass into the road. Then he ran under the car in front of us. As we were waiting and watching for the green light, the mouse was busy running back and forth between the rear wheels of the car ahead of us. He would climb up on the left rear wheel, then jump down to quickly run to the opposite wheel.

We were watching and thinking that he's gonna get squashed or smashed when the light turned green as he played beneath that car.

We became very concerned for him. Seemingly, a little innocent mouse, just playing in the street, out in a dangerous place.

However, to our delight, as the light turned green, and all the cars started moving, almost as if he knew when to stop playing in the street, he ran back into the grass. Safe and sound! We were then almost ready to applaud the little fellow! Even though he was just a mouse.

It's amazing to me at times how God, I believe, will entertain us with a small delightful event. It may be a *rainbow* after a storm or a *red bird* lighting near us in a palm tree or a *butterfly* or even a *mouse* playing in the middle of the busy street. Who would believe it?

> Our Lord, by your wisdom You made so many things, the whole earth is covered with your living creatures. (Psalm 104:24 CEV)

It is alive with creatures, large and small...
You created all of them by your Spirit. (Psalm
104:25, 30 CEV)

Learn to Do Nothing

✦◦◉◦✦

Roy McClain, who was, years ago, a pastor of the First Baptist Church in Atlanta once said that everyone should set aside *"one hour a day to do nothing."*

Just yesterday, I was saying to my son, who lives in Athens, that I was *"trying to do nothing"* when he asked me what was I doing. Then I also said that I wasn't sure I knew, in fact, how to do that.

I started working very early in life. I started paying for social security when I was only eleven. Didn't retire until I was eighty-three.

However, at the moment I was talking to him, I was sitting in my backyard. It's almost an oasis. A coy pond with fourteen brightly colored fish. Some colorful orange goldfish. Twelve palm trees. Two red cardinals visibly eating sunflower seeds. Also, squirrels darting about in the trees and on the ground.

Actually, all in all, a very serene setting. Calm. Also, with the sun shining and a cool breeze stirring.

So whether I was doing nothing or not, it was a very stress-relieving time for me. Maybe that's what doing nothing is supposed to do and be. Relief.

We know that stress will ill affect your heart and your immunity and shorten your life. So learning to be still in a calm, serene setting may be a great thing for body, mind, and spirit!

> Be still, and know that *I* am God. (Psalm 46:10 KJV)

Realize Your Terrible Time Could Be Your Door to Success

﹏✺﹏

One of the most interesting and most encouraging stories or accounts of life is that of Joseph as written in Genesis, chapter45. I suggest you read it. You may be greatly helped by it.

It reminds me of a time in my own life when I thought it was all bad, *but not so.* The tough road that I walked and experienced turned out to be and lead me to a time and life experience that was very good and successful.

If I had not gone through the rough road, I would not have experienced the good. Also, the rough road taught me to understand others who had experienced the same.

So having said that, the lesson I learned from my experience was that *a very bad experience or failure may be a door to success.* So don't discount your pain or loss today. It may mean an open door to a much better opportunity for you tomorrow.

When you read Genesis, chapter 45, verse 8, you will see Joseph's account of his own life. He explained to his bad brothers, *"So it was not you that sent me hither, but God."*

So, just remember that if you decide to give your life to God, ask Him to take charge. To guide you. Lead you. Then you can be sure that He has the power to lead you through a rough time to success.

> We know that all things work together for good, to them that love God, to them who are the called according to his purpose. (Romans 8:28 KJV)

Realize We Only Have
Two Options

∽⊙⊙∾

As you know, I read the Bible. I've read it seriously since I was fourteen years of age, beginning the Christmas of 1949 when my mother gave me my first very own and personal King James Version of the whole Bible. I have developed a habit of reading, especially the book of Proverbs daily. At least one chapter each day. And I have memorized Psalm 1, repeating it to myself often.

However, there is one passage of the Scripture that probably disturbs me most. It's Matthew 23:31–46. It deals with the final judgment. The main idea in that scripture that is so definite, so absolute, is that there are *only two options in life!* Jesus describes them as either *sheep or goats. Note strongly. There is no third option!*

There is the separation. The sheep to His right. The goats to His left. One has *good consequences. Eternal life!* One has extremely *bad consequences. Punishment forever!* There are *no halfway options!*

Lesson: All through the Bible, this is taught. We believe, or we refuse to believe. We surrender to God in humility or rebel in pride. There is good and evil. There is the wide road of unbelief and rebellion. There is the narrow road of belief and humble surrender.

In Proverbs, throughout, there are only two options. Be a *"stupid fool"* or be *"wise."* There are no other options.

> You harvest what you plant, whether good
> or bad. (Proverbs 14:14 CEV)

Wise people have enough sense to find their way but stupid fools get lost. Fools don't care if they are wrong, but God is pleased when people do right. (Proverbs 14:8–9 CEV)

Realize Your Mind, Your Heart, Often Are Discernable

✑✑✑

My wife and I were taking a walk. The day was perfect with moderate temperature in the seventies and a slight breeze. The trees were giving testimony to the gentle wind. Seemingly we were alone on the quiet street. Then a lady with her dog on a leash appeared just turning the corner.

Seeing the two of them, my wife said to the lady, "Your dog is a very contented dog."

The young lady responded with, "Yes, he is."

My wife didn't know the lady or the dog. Never had seen either of them before, yet she discerned the dog was content walking with her owner on a leash. How did my wife know the dog was content?

The truth of the matter is, many of us, maybe all of us, decide quickly, our judgment or discernment of situations, people, dogs, even places. It's a feeling we get. It's something we may not be able to completely describe or explain, but we observe it, often immediately. It may be a positive or a negative feeling. A feeling of like or dislike at first appearance. But it's real. And definite of the person, place, or thing or even animal. Some call it intuition.

Question? What do others feel or discern when they meet me or you for the first time, or second, or third? What's on the inside of us eventually shows up on our faces. Our eyes. *Who we are on the inside sooner or later becomes visible*, discernable on the outside. Our behavior. Our attitude. Our demeanor. All of these come from within our hearts!

Search me, O God, and know my heart: try me, and know my thought: and see if there be any wicked way in me and lead me in the way everlasting. (Psalm 139:23–24 KJV)

For as he thinketh in his heart, so is he. (Proverbs 23:7 KJV)

Anticipate a Wonderful Future!

❦

It was sometime in the 1990s. Gayle and I were in Vancouver, British Columbia, Canada, visiting. I was attending a seminar. I recall when I registered for the study and then bought plane tickets, I was surprised later to learn that Vancouver was across the United States in the far Northwest. The Northwest took on a whole new and different meaning to me.

Yet it was a great and far-from-home experience. So glad we went! We learned that the climate, even there, in the far Northwest was very desirable. Mild. Very little snow. Moderate temperatures all year round. Beautiful. Clean. Ocean bay. The Vancouver Bay.

New places. New experiences. New people. As one takes inventory of his memory bank, they can be such wonderful gifts to have! Especially if they were by accident. Didn't even see it coming! Life can be such a wonderful, meaningful, and adventuresome journey. Maybe it's best that we can't see far into the future. It leaves room for wonderful surprises! *As Christians, our greatest surprise is ahead of us. Heaven!*

John said:

> I saw a new heaven and a new earth. The first heaven and the first earth had disappeared and so had the sea. Then I saw New Jerusalem, that holy city, coming down from God in heaven. (Revelation 21:1, 2 KJV)

Don't Say, "If Only,"
Say, "Next Time"

⋅⋙⊚⋘⋅

This happened sometime between 1962 and 1967. I was attending a seminar in Upper State New York, sitting and having a one-on-one casual conversation with Mrs. Norman Vincent Peale. Her husband, you likely recall, was the longtime pastor of the Marble Collegiate Church in New York City and author of the famous best-selling book *The Power of Positive Thinking.*

She was telling me that actually she, herself, was more of a positive thinker than her husband. I was all ears, just listening. It was one of those special once-in-a-lifetime moments.

Nevertheless, one of the most helpful ideas that I ever gained from Dr. Peale is the thought of *Don't "If only" yourself! Think "Next time!"* Whether it was or is his original thought, I don't know.

How often do we needlessly punish ourselves with "If only I had" or "If only I hadn't" rather than realize absolutely *I can't change a single yesterday?* So parent with a wayward child? Formerly married? Anything else? *Don't "if only" yourself!*

The thief on the cross didn't look back and say, "If only." He looked forward, "And he said unto Jesus, 'Lord, remember me when Thou cometh unto Thy kingdom'" (Luke 23:42 KJV).

Convert Your Heart

❧

"*Your heart converted quickly and easily.* We didn't need all the medicine that the doctor prescribed for you." That's what the nurse said to me.

I had been admitted to the hospital the day before. So I had been there less than twenty-four hours when the nurse expressed those encouraging words.

My heartbeat was 145 when I was admitted to the hospital. My heart was out of rhythm. Not good!

Nevertheless, it was interesting to me the words she used to describe my improvement. The change from the life-threatening performance to the life-giving performance of my heart. *Converted.*

When the word *heart* is used in the Bible, it is referring to the *inner self*, not our physical heart. It has to do with our spiritual and moral being. Our consciences. Our sense of right and wrong. Our character. *Our soul.*

While it took only a few hours and a much smaller amount of medicine to convert, change, my physical heart from having bad and life-threatening performance. It may or may not take a longer time to *convert one's spiritual heart.*

Nevertheless, reading the Bible, listening to it seriously, will definitely *convert* the spiritual heart. The inner self. To spiritual life. And *save* it from spiritual death.

> Except ye be converted, and become as little children, ye shall not enter into the Kingdom of heaven. (Matthew 18:3 KJV)

> So then faith cometh by hearing and hearing by the Word of God. (Romans 10:17 KJV)

Have a Place to Call Home

~~~

We were in Chicago, Gayle and I. it was sometime in the 1990s. There we were somewhere in the city in one of the largest, highest, and most beautiful hotels. I was there to attend a psychiatric seminar.

The interesting thing and somewhat scary was the way the outside wall was in our hotel room. It was all totally glass from floor to ceiling. So it was an awesome feeling to stand near that glass wall. Clear. Solid. Visible to look down to the outside. It gave you the uncertain feeling that you might fall out. Felt like there was nothing there to hold you inside. An eerie feeling to say the least!

Consequently, we stayed several feet away from the wall. However, even from a safe distance, we could still see the water canal. The skyline. The busyness of the city. The lights at night.

I have always been glad to have visited the city that Frank Sinatra sang about as being his "kind of town." Glad that Gayle and I, together, have walked the busy sidewalks.

Yet as with a number of places I've visited, like Chicago and others, I've said, "But I wouldn't want to live here."

There's always been something special about *home*. Being home. Getting back home. There's always a bit of pain in the thoughts of "leaving home" and, worst of all, "being homeless." No roots. Hurtful to say the least. No family. Or friends. Or no purpose to be or do. Having no place to call my home. Not good!

Whether in this life or my next life, I want a home, a place to call my own.

Jesus said to His disciples:

> Don't be worried! Have faith in God and have faith in Me. I am going...to prepare a *place for each of you.* (John 14:1, 2 CEV)

Realize that Despite One's History, You Can Become

cᔆᓀᓇᔓ

As I have reported before, I was born in Rhine, Georgia, on June 6, 1935. Rhine is located in Dodge County, which is in Southeast Georgia.

Rhine and Dodge County have not always had a great reputation. It was in Rhine that Dolph Burnham, my grandfather, shot and killed a young twenty-one-year-old white man who had been married only two months. That happened on the streets of Rhine on Thursday, January 19, 1928. Later. Grandfather was acquitted after serving very little time in jail.

It was also in Rhine around 1932 that nineteen-year-old Mary Evelyn Wells, my mother-to-be, was jailed for a short time for some conflict she and her sisters got into with another woman. A physical fight happened, including hitting the other woman over the head with a bottle and pistols being pointed.

All of this history I'm sharing, just because. You can gather from it any lesson you like. They are facts in my family history. Not good, but they did really happen.

Anyway, in spite of all that, Mary Evelyn Wells married Dolph Burnham's oldest son, Warren Gaultney Burnham. Together, they became my parents.

I count my parents to have been very good parents. Dad was a very strict disciplinarian. At thirty years of age, he became a Baptist minister. My mother was a hardworking, stay-at-home, loving mother of five.

In spite of one's own past or the past of anyone's family, one can, with God's help, become not perfect but what God wants him or her to be. Believe that!

Reading the Bible helps you to become and be, especially Psalm 1 and Proverbs.

O give thanks unto the Lord; for He is good: His mercy endureth forever. (Psalm 136:1 KJV)

If we confess our sins, He is faithful and just to forgive us our sins, and to cleanse us from all unrighteousness. (**1** John 1:10 KJV)

Jesus said, "Come ye after Me, and I will make you to become fishers of men." (Mark 1:17 KJV)

Be Humble, Stay Humble

ᴄᷚᩜᷜᷜᷜ

Back in the mid-1950s, I was out of high school in my first years of college at Norman Park in South Georgia and pastoring a small country church, Kramer Baptist Church. As I said, it's small, about fifty or sixty people attending on the best Sundays.

One thing very special about those people was that they were humble folk. Not rich in material things. Small, likely hundred acres or slightly more, farmers. They dressed modestly. No fancy clothes. Often wore overalls, not just to work in the fields but often to church. That was their Sunday best.

They moved about without the rush of city folk. They sat on their porches and talked with one another as families. Shared and helped with their neighbors. Took time to visit one another.

Many things I learned from them! Though most weren't college educated, they were wise, not arrogant, humble, lots of common sense kind of people.

They knew like Forest Gump would say, *"What love was."*

That period of my life will always be remembered as a foundation-building time of my life. I was only in my twenties. I'm so blessed to have been given and taught so much by those wonderful people! *Humble! Very wise!*

Wise people are humble people! Not arrogant.

> With all my heart I praise You, Lord in the presence of angels I sing your praises. Though You are above us all. *You care for humble people.* (Psalm 138:1, 6 CEV)

> There is more hope for a fool than for someone who says, I'm really smart! (Proverbs 26:12 CEV)

Remember the Bible
Speaks Your Language

{ornament}

It was sometime in the 1990s. That was the decade that Gayle and I did most of our traveling to faraway places, distant cities. This time, we were visiting Quebec, Canada. We had been to Vancouver, British Columbia, but this was our first and only visit to Quebec.

One thing that made Quebec so unique was it was the only place we ever visited where English was not their everyday language. They did speak English but usually spoke French.

Gayle and I enjoyed being there walking the streets, eating in the restaurants, and seeing the beautiful gothic church buildings. They too were different. Reminded me somewhat of St. Patrick Cathedral, a Catholic church in New York City.

Nevertheless, one special moment I recall was when we were seated in a restaurant, about to order our meal, thinking, *How can we do this in a French-speaking country?* The waitress quickly made known to me that she could speak English too. It was a nice and pleasant surprise to me that she could meet me where I was. Speak my language.

Lesson to be reminded of: The Bible, God's Word, can meet you where you are. Reading Proverbs and Psalms, you often think, the writer is reading my mind and knows how I feel. *Speaking my language!*

> You have looked deep into my heart, Lord,
> and *you know all about me.* You know when I am
> resting or when I am working, and from heaven
> *You discover my thoughts.* (Psalm 139:1–2 CEV)

You Can Do It

⚜

S he was my fourth-grade teacher. Several of us had not been doing very well on our testing. Not studying enough. So she said in somewhat of a threatening tone, "If any of you fail this test tomorrow, I'm going to paddle you."

She knew we were capable. Now remember, this was 1944. I was only a mere nine-year-old kid. The ruling back then was a million miles from today, 2020. Then the understanding was, "If you get a spanking at school, you'll get another one when you get home." The school and the home were very much together. No questions asked. No arguing between child and parent. The teacher, with the parents' consent, was always right.

Nevertheless, the next day for the test came. About six or seven of us failed the test and received the consequences. Knowing the unwritten but agreed-upon rule between teacher and parent, I never told my parents. Never!

I learned early in life, then and on and on, that *I individually was responsible for my success or failure. No blaming someone else!* Thus, I did take on and accept fully that responsibility!

Admittedly, that time and era, the 1940s and 1950s, was a golden era for families raising children. There was a wise, very commonsense relationship among parents, teachers, and children that was extremely good. The greatest winner was the child!

Whether you buy into the idea of spanking or not, it's extremely important to learn and to teach that the *individual*, even from childhood, is *responsible* for his or her own behavior and thoughts. Success or failure!

> I *can* do all things *through Christ* which strengtheneth *me*. (Philippians 4:13 KJV)

Reading the Bible daily, especially Psalm 1 and Proverbs, helps and encourages you to believe in yourself! You can do it! You can be wise! You can succeed!

Be Like a Healthy Tree

※⑥⑤⑥

We have this very, very tall pine tree on our property. There is bad news about the tree. It is different from the several trees that stand nearby. It is dead.

No one has had to inform me that the tree is dead. It is very noticeable even to my eyes. Several other, just ordinary people, not scientists, have looked and quickly concluded that the tree, though very tall, is dead.

Since it is dead, they, like myself, have concluded that the tree is dangerous. A storm could easily cause it to fall crashing against my neighbor's house.

So we have decided that the dangerous dead tree should be cut down and removed. Not only does it no longer have any worthwhile purpose. Its very existence and presence are negative. It could fall, caused by even a minor wind, and do severe damage.

Note that the tree has only two options for existence. Live! Stand tall! Endure the inevitable winds! Contribute to the environment as healthy trees do, or be dead and dangerous—one a positive, the other a negative.

So is a human life. Positive or negative. One may give and give. Being generous to the environment, to society. His family. Even to himself. Or a person may choose to be dead and dangerous to all those around and even to themself. Like a dead tree. Worthless.

Note there is one major difference. The tree had no choice. It was the victim of insects likely. *People* choose to be positive or negative. *Worthwhile* or *worthless! Then God decides the consequences!*

> Blessed is the man that...his delight is in
> the law of the Lord; and in his law doth he medi-
> tate day and night...he shall be like a tree planted

by the rivers of water, that bringeth forth his fruit in his season; his leaf also shall not wither; and whatsoever he doeth shall prosper. The ungodly are not so; but are like the chaff which the wind driveth away. (Psalm 1:1–4 KJV)

Stay in Touch with Friends

Yesterday, July 28, 2020, I made a phone call to a friend, in fact, two friends, whom I have known for roughly fifty years. I knew both of them when we all lived in Maryland in the 1960s and 1970s and even into the 1980s. I knew one of them, John Woodall, when we both lived in Pennsylvania. He lived in Chambersburg. I lived in Carlisle.

John now lives in Alabama, and my other friend, Burnis Barrett, lives in Frederick, Maryland. John is almost eighty years old. Burnis is eighty-eight. John's mind is waning. Burnis's body, he says, is waning. Weaker. Walks with a cane. Vision is less than it once was. He lives alone, a widower.

Why do I stay in touch with these guys? Why have I initiated the call from time to time through the years? Several reasons. Both guys are and have always been so genuine. Real. Honest. Friends. I have always been encouraged by them. I always felt free to be myself with them. And usually gotten a laugh just talking with them. Even now as all three of our lives wane.

> Some friends don't help, but a true friend is closer than your own family. Proverbs 18:24 CEV

Realize Both Are True—I Don't Know and I Do Know

❧☙

It was sometimes during the decade of the 1990s. Gayle and I were in New Orleans. We had lived there in 1959–1962 while I was a student at New Orleans Baptist Theological Seminary. Both of our girls, Linda and Dianne, were born there.

But this time in the 1990s, we were just visiting, staying in one of the beautiful hotels. I was attending a psychiatric seminar. So sitting in a session one day, taught by a Harvard professor, I heard the professor answer a question from another class participant with, "I don't know." He had already answered many difficult questions from several of my peers, but then with this particular problem and question, he slightly bowed his head, eyes seemingly looking at nothing, with a paused demeanor, questioning his own mind, searching for an answer. He said, "*I don't know.* I'll have to do some research on that."

How often is life like that? One may be the most knowledgeable, learned, intelligent. But life happens! The personal, human, honest answer is, *I don't know.* I don't know what to do. I don't know what to say. It's a pause time. A searching of the mind, the heart. Still, all we can come up with, if we're honest, is *I don't know!* That's why we need faith, in God!

> Now all we can see of God is like a cloudy picture in a mirror, later we will see Him face to face. *We don't know everything, but then we will,* just as God completely understands us. (1 Corinthians 13:12 CEV)

The apostle Paul said:

> We know that all things work together for good to them that love God, to them who are the called according to His purpose. (Romans 8:28 KJV)

Reading the Bible, especially Psalm 1 and Proverbs, helps us to know what we need to know. Even though we'll never know it all.

Maintenance, Absolutely Necessary

༄ঔৎৎঔ

The maintenance factor: Someone might ask the question, "*Why should I read* and *meditate* on the Bible, especially Proverbs and Psalms, *every day?*"

It's about like asking, "Why should I have to maintain a car? I've already bought and paid for it." But the fact of wear and tear is now involved. On the road, there is a danger of collision, damage. There is the wear and tear of use. Weather. Mileage on the engine, the tires, the transmission.

As there is wear and tear on a car, even more so on our lives, our brains, our thoughts, our attitudes, and our contentment or the lack thereof.

The daily wear and tear on you are much greater than on a vehicle!

That's why we need to read and meditate on the Bible every day. You, we, cannot escape the wear and tear on our brain, our minds, our thoughts, every day. We need the maintenance factor. Reading. Thinking. Absorbing Bible truths for direction. Instructions. Guidance. Encouragement. *More wisdom!* We all need *daily* help!

> God blesses everyone who has wisdom and common sense. (Proverbs 3:13 CEV)

> My soul melteth for heaviness; strengthen thou me according unto thy Word. (Psalm 119:28 KJV)

Read, Meditate on Psalm 91

There are some passages of the Scripture that speak to me in a special and powerful way, more so than others, at times. They are likely just more relevant at times in my life. Perhaps I need certain scriptures at certain times.

I find Psalm 91 one of those scriptures. I have been brought back to it again and again. I have recently memorized verses 1 and 11.

> He that dwelleth in the secret place of the Most High shall abide under the shadow of the Almighty. (Psalm 91:1 KJV)

> For He shall give His angels charge over thee, to keep thee in all thy ways. (Psalm 91:11 KJV)

Reading, memorizing, and meditating on scriptures is a way of *encouraging yourself.* Learning to encourage yourself is a very wise and basic principle to *practice* in order to feed your mind, your Spirit, and your soul.

Don't depend on others to do it for you. *Learn to feed yourself!* Act and live like a *wise* mature adult!

> When we were children, we thought and reasoned as children do. But when we grew up, we quit our childish ways. (1 Corinthians 13:11 CEV)

> Thy word is a lamp unto my feet, and a light unto my path. (Psalm 119:105 KJV)

Keep Prodding Day by Day

❧❧❧

It was in the 1940s, probably 1945 or 1946, when my brother Larry, Delton, our uncle, and I were outside at my grandfather's farm near Rhine. We were watching a mule walk around and around in the same path grinding the sugarcane into juice. The mule walked slowly, never increasing his speed to a gloppy. Same slow monotonous walk for hour after hour in the hot sun all day long.

The green cane juice would later be placed in a thick iron, very large container with a hot blazing fire beneath. The results would be a sweet thick syrup.

The sugarcane syrup would then make its way to a gallon metal container and then to Grandmother's breakfast table to be served every morning. With the syrup, would be the best homemade biscuits, cooked on a woodburning stove. With the biscuits, butter, and syrup, would be ground grits, not creamy, smooth like we have in 2020. Also, there would be fried or scrambled eggs and bacon. Delicious would not even come close to describing that country, farm breakfast.

But the one thing that has stood out in my memory for years and years is that syrup!

Never have I been able, as an adult, to find anywhere a syrup like Grandmother's. I'll always feel indebted to that mule. The syrup was the product of his very slow, monotonous walking to grind out that cane juice.

Lesson: So much of life is slow. Walking. Routine. Prodding. Maybe even monotonous, day after day, the same path. Sometimes you may not realize how productive you are. *I'm fairly sure that mule never realized how productive he was. But he was!*

> And let us not be weary in well doing;
> for in due season we shall reap, if we faint not.
> (Galatians 6:9 KJV)

Gain Peace and Strength

⚙️

This morning, I was reading a devotional book. Alone in our den, everything quiet, no sounds except the quietness. Couldn't hear the birds singing out our back door. Couldn't hear the squirrels scrambling and chasing one another. Couldn't even see or hear our one frog diving into our pond. Couldn't see or hear the fish splashing water, swimming in our small ten-by-ten goldfish pond. Couldn't even hear the white water rushing across the rocks into the pond.

So when I say quiet, I do mean it was quiet. You could almost hear the silence; it was so still and motionless.

But then I read from my devotional book, *"The Lord will give strength to His people; the Lord will bless His people with peace"* (Psalm 29:11 KJV). It seemed to break into the silence. It spoke loudly to me of two things: strength in body and peace in mind. Both were from God. Both were needed daily.

So I prayed, asking God to give me both. Like daily bread and quietness. To be able to shut out of my mind the noisy circumstances of a very troubled country and world. At least for a while.

Only God can help us to have strength and peace. To be able to close the doors of our mind to the unnecessary and troubling noise of a chaotic world that we may have peace in our mind and strength to endure in our body. Read. The Bible. Daily. Psalm 23.

> Be of good courage, and He shall strengthen your heart, all ye that hope in the Lord. (Psalm 31:24 KJV)

Believe, Why I Personally Believe

୧୨୧

One father told me that his two sons were now atheists. Another father told me that one of his children had become an agnostic.

Although both of the fathers (families) were devoted Christians and active church members, these children had decided, as adults, to be unbelievers. How this could happen, I have no idea. No answers. Trying to give a neat theological or parental circumstantial answer to that would be like giving a neat answer to, Why did Adam and Eve rebel against God when they had it so good in the Garden of Eden?

It was their decision! It was not God's fault! He did nothing wrong to cause it. It was their freedom to decide. They had the freedom to rebel.

But hearing these stories of these fathers and their children, I ask myself, *Why do I personally believe in God?*

I could generally say, "Because I believe the Bible." And I do. But that is somewhat of a generic answer. But why, more personally?

My answer is that I have personally experienced several, if not many, times that *God has helped me personally* out of very difficult situations. When I was down, flat on my face, or flat on my back. In a few times of loss and failure. Times of very, very challenging situations. *He answered my very personal cry for help.* That's why I believe!

> I waited patiently for the Lord; and He inclined unto me, and heard my cry. (Psalm 40:1 KJV)

> I love You Lord! You answered my prayers. You paid attention to me. (Psalm 116:1, 2 CEV)

Make New Friends
with Good People

‿◦◯◦‿

N ever had I ever seen him before. He was a blue-collar service-man who was talking to me in my front yard.

But I soon felt a sense of friendship, especially after he began to share with me so openly and honestly about his life and past. He told me that he had not been married long and was forty-two years of age. Recently retired from the military, the Army, after serving twenty-one years. Had been deployed to Iraq and Afghanistan several times. Was a demolition expert. Knew how to make bombs and blow up buildings and knew how to defuse the bombs.

Not only could I hear his goodness, but I could also feel it as he continued to share not only his accomplishments but also his weaknesses.

Those are the characteristics of a good and great man. Acknowledging his strengths and his weaknesses. Being so honest with himself.

I volunteered to him saying, "You are a good man." I said it emphatically. He thanked me.

I meant it! I also told him that I personally felt indebted to him because I have never served in the military.

It's a blessing. A gift to meet new people, especially good people! Great people like this young man. And I told him, admittedly with some tears, that he, in those few minutes, had been a blessing to me. Again, he thanked me. Although so different in age. He was forty-two; me, eighty-five. Different in eras of a lifetime. In past experiences. In race. Yet our hearts met as friends.

> The words of a good person are like pure silver. (Proverbs 10:20 CEV)

> Good people are like trees with deep roots. (Proverbs 12:12 CEV)

> Good people have kind thoughts. (Proverbs 12:5 CEV)

We Need the "No Matter What" Factor

❧◦◦◦◦❧

This morning reading the Bible, I discovered a verse in Psalm 119 (CEV), the longest chapter in the Bible, that I had never noticed before—verse 112. *"I have made up my mind to obey Your laws forever no matter what"* (Psalm 119 CEV). The *"no matter what"* phrase was what caught my attention.

The verse is regarding a decision to obey God. *"No matter what."*

The fact is that every important decision in life needs the "no matter what" fact to be firm, lasting, definite, and authentic. Truth is that keeping the decision may "not be easy." May not "feel like it." *The fact is that most important decisions in life are not easy!*

Staying on the job. Working day after day. Marriage. Raising a child. Getting an education. Being a Christian. Living a Christian life. Obeying God. Doing the right thing. Not easy. May, at times, just don't feel like it.

So like the psalmist, we need to make up our minds (decide) to obey and stay at it (the important things) "no matter what"!

> Although the fig tree shall not blossom, neither shall fruit be on the vines; the labor of the olive shall fail, and the fields shall yield me no meat; the flock shall be cut off from the fold, and there shall be no herd in the stalls; yet I will rejoice in the Lord, I will joy in the God of my Salvation. (Habakkuk 3:17–18 KJV)

Read the Bible Daily, Especially Proverbs

After having had two careers in my lifetime, over thirty years as a Baptist minister, I was privileged to serve in Pennsylvania, Maryland, Louisiana, and Georgia. Then working in private practice as a psychotherapist for twenty-eight years.

The one thing that has amazed me through the years is the *lack of wisdom*. Said perhaps better would be the *lack of common sense.*

In recent years, I have often said and been made to believe that unfortunately and sadly common sense, wisdom, is no longer common even among some of the most well-educated, college-, and university-degreed people.

Of course, you only need to read and watch the daily news stories to conclude the same. There is a pitiful, sad, and destructive lack of common sense (wisdom).

Why is there such a lack of (wisdom) common sense today? One simple reason!

The lack of reading the Bible. By reading the Bible, especially Proverbs. Thinking seriously about it. Meditating daily on it. *You* may gain *wisdom. Good common sense!*

> All wisdom comes from the Lord and so do common sense and understanding. (Proverbs 2:6 CEV)

Look Beyond the Grave

❧

The time was about 2006. Amy, our granddaughter, was six or seven years of age. I had finished a somewhat extended conversation with her of biblical or theological truths about God and salvation.

So then thinking I had been very thorough with my explaining and teaching, I asked her, "So, Amy, now what do we have to do in order to get to heaven?"

She, without pause, said, "We have to die."

Admittedly, it wasn't the answer I was expecting. But her answer hit hard and was absolutely true. We have to die.

Dying is not an option. It's not left up to us to decide. Do I want to die or not? We will die! Sooner or later. That day will come. Must come! It's part of the plan for our lives. We're born. We live a while. We die.

We plan for the here and now. We need to plan for our eternal future. It's much longer. *We need to look beyond the grave. Think about it. Living here and now forever is not an option!* We must die in order to get into eternity. Just like Amy said.

> Our bodies are gradually dying… Things that are seen don't last forever, but things that are not seen are eternal. That's why we need to keep our minds on the things that cannot be seen. (2 Corinthians 4:16, 18 CEV)

Let Your Caring Happen

෴

A few days ago, I was thinking of buying and giving a gift—in fact, a nice shirt that I like—for one of my sons-in-law. Just because I was considering recently how very good he has been to my daughter and grandchildren.

Then my idea was, I felt, shot down when my wife suggested that I do the same for one of our sons. My immediate thought was *I should not have shared my thought. Just done it.*

What about the idea of doing something for one person without doing the same for others, perhaps several others?

The fact of the matter is, we have not treated all of our children, their spouses, and their children, our grandchildren, equally. No, we haven't.

Is that okay? Is it okay to think singularly at times? Another fact is that we can't do it all. For reason after reason. We can't or don't treat them all the same. They are not the same. Their needs are not the same. Circumstances are not the same.

So is it okay? Is it fair? Reasonable? To at times just do something for someone. *Just because you want to at the moment? Spontaneously.* Singularly. Not their birthday. Not Christmas. Without feeling you have to include everybody.

I think so. I hope so. I believe so. I've done it a few times, if not many. I once bought my wife a diamond ring *just because.* Not her birthday. Not anniversary. Not Christmas. *Just because!*

Love and caring for one another are not always logical. It's spontaneous from the heart!

> Jesus was in the town of Bethany… A woman came in with a bottle of expensive perfume and poured it on Jesus's head…but when

his disciples saw this they became angry and complained, "Why such a waste?" Jesus said…, *She has done a beautiful thing for me.*" (Matthew 26:6, 7, 8, 10 CEV)

Realize You Can Have a
Wonderful Experience

e√☺☺☺☻

"Warren and I went plum picking. We had a heart-to-heart talk and had a *wonderful experience*."

That is what Gayle wrote in her diary on June 5, 1956. She was nineteen years old. I was twenty. We had known each other since the fall of 1954.

I don't recall what the "heart-to-heart talk" was about, nor do I remember anything about the "wonderful experience."

I can assure you the interpretation of these words likely depend on the era of your upbringing. To us, it might have meant a hug or a kiss. But actually, I know it wasn't even that because I know that I didn't even kiss her the first year we dated. And there was no intimacy until after we said, "I do," in marriage on June 5, 1957.

So what was the "wonderful experience"? My guess is that she meant our presence with each other. The ability to look into each other's eyes. To talk. To share thoughts and feelings.

Unfortunately, for so many in this era, the twenty-first century, it's a lost art. A lost "wonderful experience." But you can have it if you seek God. His will. His purpose for your life. *Early! In your youth!*

> *Remember now thy Creator in the days of thy youth* while the evil days come not, nor the years draw nigh, when thou shalt say, I have no pleasure in them. (Ecclesiastes 12:1 KJV)

> Flee also youthful lusts: but follow righteousness, faith, charity, peace, with them that call on the Lord out of a pure heart. (2 Timothy 2:22 KJV)

Accept Your Loss and Go On

᭯᭢᭠

It was 1982. I was living in Maryland with my family. Had a good job that I enjoyed and loved. Then seemingly almost suddenly, I resigned from the job and took a job in Georgia. Thinking I was going back home. It felt like a tremendous loss. I grieved a great deal. It was and has been through the years difficult for me to accept the loss and move on.

It was a pastorate I gave up. It has been strangely a struggle to feel totally at home in any church since then.

That's not a good story for anyone. Many people, millions and millions, have lost something dear to them for one reason or another. Maybe the death of a child, a spouse, or a parent. A relationship. Divorce. Job. Place. Whatever. But losses happen.

Learning to *accept a loss and go on* is probably for many people an extremely needed lesson to learn. Accepting a loss though it may leave a scar on your heart, your emotions, for a lifetime. *It Is possible to accept a heartbreaking loss and keep on living.*

The apostle Paul spoke of *"forgetting those things which are behind, and reaching forth unto those things which are before"* (Philippians 3:13 KJV)

The Lord spoke unto Joshua, "Moses my servant is dead; now *therefore arise, go over* this Jordan"(Joshua 1:2).

> Jesus said, "Let not your heart be troubled:
> You believe in God believe also in me." (John
> 14:1 KJV)

Go On Down the Road

❦

A few years ago, there was a frequent commercial on television advertising a car battery. The final words were to put the new battery in your vehicle and just *"go on down the road."*

Sometimes in life, it's not easy to just *"go on down the road."* It may have to do with a job, or a place, or a relationship. We don't want to be called or feel like a quitter. So we hold onto something, a place, a work, or even a person, which is no longer healthy or best for everyone concerned. No use in beating a dead horse so to speak. But again, it's hard for us to turn loose. "Am I giving up, or am I a quitter?" we ask ourselves.

The truth of the matter is, there may come the moment when it's time to *just go on down the road.* Have a new start. A fresh beginning. Find new ground to plant your life. Your time. Your energy. You may be trying to force the seed of your life to grow in rock-solid soil. Fertile soil does exist! Find it! Just *"go on down the road."*

> After the death of Moses the servant of the Lord, the Lord said to Joshua... Moses my servant is dead; now therefore arise go over this Jordan, you and all this people, into a land which I am giving to them. (Joshua 1:1–2 KJV)

Consider the Squirrels,
the Fish, the Birds

It was a regular morning in early September. Glad to feel that the hot blazing 90-plus degree summer was slowly coming to an end. Fall temperatures were on the promising horizon.

So there I sat in my backyard, soaking up my environment like a sponge.

The fish, thirty of them, swam in my goldfish pond. The birds, especially the red birds, cardinals. Two of them, male and female. The scrambling furry squirrels, I can often see four or five at the same time. The majestic pine trees stood over a hundred feet tall. The thirteen palm trees were all within view. The emerald-green lily pads floated quietly on the pond. The beautiful, even gorgeous bright-yellow lily standing taller in the midst of the lily pads.

Also, the ability to see and hear the water rushing over the rocks down into the pond. And I can hear and feel the wind blowing. Not harsh. Just a soft breeze, but audible.

So I consider myself rich when I can see and hear all these. So to speak, "take it all in," soak it into my heart. My soul. My being. It feeds my spirit.

So I remind myself of the environment that God has given me, especially when a sense of anxiety, loneliness, or meaninglessness tries to rob me of contentment, hope, and peace.

When I'm tempted to look and think too much of circumstances and events beyond my control, I try to consider what squirrels, birds, or fish may be worried about. *I think. Not much!*

Jesus said:

> I tell you not to worry about your life...
> Look at the birds in the sky... Your Father in
> heaven takes care of them. Aren't you worth more
> than birds? Why do you have such little faith?
> (Matthew 6:25–26, 32, 30 CEV)

Be Prepared to Die Like Andy

ᥦᥩᥩᥬ

"He is about to die. We only expect him to last a few more hours. We are already planning his funeral." The voice was an early morning phone call to me. Those were the words of Rusty, the grown son, referring to his eighty-six-year-old father in University Hospital. I offered to come to the hospital to see them. He suggested I not. "He's already unconscious," he said. "No use."

Within a short while, the funeral director called me, informing me of the funeral plans.

Andy was one of those special people. A quiet man of few words, always positive, and has a contagious smile. Even his own wife and family said, "He never complained." They spoke of him as a *"genuine Christian."*

Death will finally come to all of us, whether we're good or bad, causing sorrow to family and friends!

Reading the Bible daily helps to prepare us for death, whether it's a loved one or our own.

> Blessed are the dead which die in the Lord
> from henceforth: yea saith the Spirit, that they
> may rest from their labours; and their works do
> follow them. (Revelation 14:13 KJV)

Realize Good Places and Good People Encourage You

eෙⓄ๑ৎ

There we were. It was a beautiful sunny day on the Chesapeake Bay. Water, water everywhere. We were on a small yacht. As you may know, the Chesapeake Bay is a waterway between Maryland and Virginia. At one time, it was a great source of fish, oysters, and crabs.

Crisfield, Maryland, where we lived in 1967–1972, located on the Bay, was once known as the Crab Capital of the World. Crisfield, her past, was famous for seafood.

Nevertheless, this day, as earlier mentioned, was a special day for Gayle and me, being escorted out on a fishing trip in the middle of the bay. Fishing for trout in very deep water. The great thing about the adventure was that we actually caught some fish. We were enjoying the company of some warm friendly people. They were so kind, thoughtful, appreciative, and accepting of us. That was the way it was on the Eastern Shore of Maryland for all six of our family.

The truth of the matter was that each and every day for five consecutive years was special. Beautiful. Sunny. Whether we were out fishing with the people or just visiting in their homes.

Lesson point: It's good to frequent good places and good people who are friendly and accepting of you. You can feel the atmosphere that encourages you and lightens your heart!

> Wise friends make you wise, but you hurt yourself by going around with fools. (Proverbs 13:20 CEV)

Learn from Wise Examples

⟨⟨⟨⟨⟨⟩⟩⟩⟩⟩

When I was only twenty-seven years of age, I moved from New Orleans to Carlisle, Pennsylvania, with my wife, Gayle, and our two small daughters: Linda, age three, and Sheila Dianne, age one. The year was 1962. John F. Kennedy was President.

While there, I learned of the Army War College in Carlisle. Originally, it was a school for American Indians. The famous Jim Thorpe attended the Indian school.

But in regard to the Army War College, the students are colonels or lieutenant colonels. As a young pastor of the Carlisle Baptist Church, I visited several of the officers' homes. These were Army officers. Successful to say the least. Forty percent of the class would become generals.

The thing that caught my attention about these men was that they *were not arrogant. Humble-minded* men. *Wise. Often men of faith.*

They accepted me into their homes, in spite of my youth, and let me pray with them. They were teachable, not "know-it-alls!"

Point to consider: Wise men. Successful men. Men of faith. They are teachable. Question! Do you want to be that kind of person?

Reading and learning Psalm 1 and the book of Proverbs, daily, thinking about the words, will *help you* be that kind of person. Think about it! That's my desire and goal for you! For myself also!

> Blessed is the man that walketh not in the counsel of the ungodly…but his delight is in the law of the Lord; and in his law doth he meditate day and night…and whatsoever he doeth shall prosper. (Psalm 1:1–3 KJV)

Pray for Yourself

Someone told me a story of a man who, over and over, prayed in church out loud for God to remove the spiderwebs from the church. He was not speaking literally but symbolically. Not in a positive mindset. Referring to the lack of any evidence of spiritual power as being like spiderwebs.

Week after week, Sunday after Sunday, he prayed verbally for all to hear, for God to remove the spiderwebs. On one Sunday, a quiet fellow church member interrupted the man's prayer, yelling, "God, please just kill the spider." Whether the story was true or not, I do not know.

However, often our prayers may become monotonous. Not clear. Not specific. Not definite. Like webs. So spread out. Hanging. I am reminded of the psalmist who prayed so definitely. Even singularly. Very personal.

> Look deep into my heart, God, and find out everything I am thinking. Don't let me follow evil ways, but lead me in the way that time has proven true. (Psalm 139:23–24 CEV)

> Let my words and my thoughts be pleasing to you Lord, because You are my mighty rock and my protector. (Psalm 19:14)

Read and Reread Joshua
Chapter One

ᶜᵒ☙◉☙ᵒ

O ne of my favorite chapters in the Bible is Joshua chapter 1. It tells of God speaking personally to Joshua, acknowledging the death of Moses, then telling Joshua, "I'm looking to you now, Joshua. It's your job now to lead the children of Israel into the promised land." God informed Joshua that it was his task to continue their journey and cross over the Jordan River. Then God said, *"As I was with Moses, so I will be with thee: I will not fail thee, nor forsake thee"* (Joshua 1:5b KJV)

> Only be thou strong and very courageous that thou mayest observe to do according to all the law, which Moses my servant commanded thee: turn not from it to the right hand or to the left that thou mayest prosper whithersoever thou goest. (Joshua 1:7 KJV)

I have read over and over many times Joshua chapter 1. *It has been very encouraging to me. I hope you too will read it often.*

Live Right

⌒⌒⌒

As a pastor and psychotherapist for over sixty years, I have listened privately and personally to thousands of hours of some heartbreaking stories. I have heard and seen the truth of some scriptures lived out in life, in the here and now. Consider these scriptures.

> *God let* these people go their own way. (Romans 1:24 CEV)

> Since these people refused even to think about God, He let their useless minds rule over them. (Romans 1:28 CEV)

The bottom line is God lets us have what we want even though it may be personal suicide.

The best way to look out for yourself, to truly love yourself, is to realize that God's way is the best way for you. He loves you more than the devil. More than evil. More than wrong.

Sin may look pleasurable, but it actually is self-destructive. And none of us are islands. When one chooses evil, he or she usually carries others along. One person's wrong choices hurt so many others. Break hearts. So many tears!

> Live right, and you are safe! But sin will destroy you. (Proverbs 13:6 CEV)

Stop before It Is Too Late

❧◍◐◔

It was a tragedy about to happen. The train engineer wanted to stop his train, but he couldn't. It was too late. He had just come up a slight hill, going west from the Ocmulgee River. Now his speed was faster and increasing as he came under the highway bridge, near our home in Abbeville, Georgia.

Suddenly, shockingly, unexpectedly, the engineer saw a sight that terrified him. There, just several yards in front of him on the track, between the tracks, was a child, a toddler. How did he wander away from his home, his parents, just a short distance from the tracks? But there he was, alone, unaware of what was about to happen to him within seconds.

This truly happened about two hundred yards from where we lived in the late 1940s. I was a teenager.

Note. There are times in one's life when he or she needs to stop something, maybe a behavior. If he or she doesn't, the one to die early is self. Not someone else. Self-destruction! *The longer we go and the faster in one direction, the harder it is to stop!*

Jesus said:

> I tell you, Nay; but, except ye repent, ye shall all likewise perish. (Luke 13:5 KJV)

> You can be sure that if you don't turn back to God, everyone of you will also die. (Luke 13:5 CEV)

Absolutely Seek Wisdom
as You Age

~∞~

One of the main memories of my paternal grandfather, Dolph Burnham, was seeing him sitting in his rocking chair on the wrap-around front porch, out in the country, near Rhine, Georgia. He always had a five-foot-long switch broken from a peach tree limb. He used it to kill flies in the South Georgia hot summertime.

That was when my brother, Larry, and I stayed with them, the three summers, June, July, and August, of 1943, 1944, and 1945. At that time, he was in his sixties, born in 1880.

In earlier days, when his own kids were still at home, he had a reputation of coming home some nights on a "mean drunk," causing Grandmother to fearfully take their kids and hide out in the corn-field behind their house.

He and all four of his brothers, except for one, were said to have killed at least one person during their lifetime.

As a young kid, all I knew him to kill were flies, sitting in his rocking chair. Calm. Soft-spoken. Perhaps tamed by the wear and tear of his earlier years.

It was said that he was converted to the faith. Faith in Christ before he died. I only hope the conversion story is true.

> The days of our years are three score years and ten: So teach us to number our days, that we may apply our hearts unto wisdom. (Psalm 90:10, 12 KJV)

Remember Your Yesteryears

⤜⤛⟲⤚⤝

Larry, my younger brother, Mom and Dad's second child, was about eight or nine years of age when this happened. I was sixteen months older, about ten or eleven. Both of us were preteens. Walking on our way home, from Mr. Tom Sapp's grocery store, where Dad had a charge account. Mom would often send Larry and me with a grocery list errand. Just the two of us. We could walk to Abbeville's uptown. It was only about fifteen minutes from our house. There was no car in our family.

So on this sunny summer day, Mother had sent us to town for one single item. One roll of toilet paper. Not kidding. So Larry and I were on our way home. Mission accomplished. Carrying the roll of toilet paper, suddenly becoming aware of how silly that may seem or look to someone. Maybe one of our friends, seeing us with the single item. Exposed. Not in a bag. So we started tossing the roll back and forth.

"You carry it."

"No, you carry it!"

Like a baseball.

I forget who finally carried it home and handed the roll of paper to Mom. Why would my mother send her two very mischievous boys on such an errand? Don't know. However, it's a humorous memory.

And that was life for us. Poor, in a small town, in the mid-1940s.

> But thou shalt remember the Lord thy God:
> for it is He that giveth thee power to get wealth.
> (Deuteronomy 8:18 KJV)

Learn Early with Your
Hands and Your Heart

᯾ᯖᯅᯖᯅᯌ

M r. Sapp's grocery store in Abbeville, Georgia, was a significant learning place for me during my eleventh, twelfth, and thirteenth years in 1946, 1947, and 1948. Those were the days and years immediately after World War II. Great years of peace, quiet, and thankfulness.

They were also simple years. Not only very ordinary but also great years.

One significant thing I remember was those were the years before prepackaging. You didn't come into a grocery store and find meat or cheese prepackaged at Mr. Sapp's store.

As a young clerk, I learned to cut up a chicken, the whole chicken, for the customer. If the customer wanted beef steak, I would go to the large refrigerator, take down from a hook a quarter of a cow, and cut off one or more steaks. I also learned to cut exactly (almost) a pound of cheese from a large round of cheese.

None of these were prepackaged, ready to be picked up from a showcase as they are today.

So there was this conversation that happened between the clerk (me) and the customer before the purchase. It was a learning time for me. A personal time between people. Communicating face-to-face.

Point. *It's extremely wise to begin learning to do good things with your hands and your heart early in life.*

> From a child thou hast know the Holy
> Scriptures, which are able to make thee wise unto
> salvation through faith which is in Christ Jesus.
> (2 Timothy 3:15 KJV)

Consider the Strong Trees

✑✑✑✑

O ne of the things that I vividly remember about my homeplace, where I grew up in 1941–1953, was the trees in our yard.

Of course, there was no grass in our yard. It was just dirt on all four sides of the house. Any grass that sprouted, we would just pull it up.

In front of the house was this large oak tree. Big. In the backyard were two fig trees and a couple of pecan trees. But there was one tree that seemingly was so worthless yet special. We called it a chinaberry tree. It was so different. So few of them. Rare. No claim for fame, but it was there, located on the back south corner of our house.

When I visualize my childhood home, I always see those trees. We climbed them. Played in their shade in the summertime. Ate the figs and pecans in the fall. Worked under them, raking up their leaves in the fall and winter.

Our yard was our playground. The trees were never to be disturbed or broken by any southern ice storm. Never were injured by any disease. Stood stalwart every year I lived there for twelve years, 1941–1953.

It's interesting and somewhat amazing that good people, people of God, are often compared to strong-rooted trees.

God blesses these people who refuse evil advice and won't follow sinners or join in sneering at God. Instead, they find happiness in the teachings of the Lord, and they think about it day and night (Psalm 1:1–2 CEV).

> They are like trees growing beside a stream,
> trees that produce fruit in season and always have
> leaves. Those people succeed in everything they
> do. (Psalm 1:3 CEV)

Hopefully We Mellow
as We Grow Older

This happened sometime near or about 1984. I had come from near Savannah to Eastman to spend time with Mom and Dad. He at that time was seventy-three, and I was forty-nine. We were out walking together in one of his two gardens. It was a warm, sunny day. Casual time.

The significant thing about our time together was that it was casual. It was a mellow time between father and son. Two adults.

From my perspective, it was a first! Growing up, I had never felt that warmth between us. My memory and feelings of former days were different. Not close, certainly not warm. Honestly, I felt fear of him. Definite respect. But that was about it. Not what I was feeling at forty-nine years of age.

Until he died, years later, in 1997. I was and am grateful to have continued those good feelings. Warmth. Even now that he's gone, I still have them.

Frankly, knowing some of how he grew up. Born in 1911. Tough, stern, rough, sparse. Hard times wouldn't come close to describing his own early years. I have great respect and appreciation for his ability to finally mellow and soften in his older years.

> For now there are faith, hope and love. But
> of these three, the greatest is love. (1 Corinthians
> 13:13 CEV)

Read Bible Daily with Your Young Children

ᴄᴏᴏᴏᴏᴏ

I wrote this article (Our Alan) in 1985, thirty-five years ago, about our son.

It was a Monday that we had received two letters from Alan who was at Parris Island South Carolina in basic training with the Marines. The letters were the kind every parent loves to receive from a child their first time away from home. Of course, Gayle and I have been concerned for him, praying for him every day. *Well, the letters revealed some of his heart. He said that he was reading one or two chapters in Psalms every evening. Praying. Repeating Scripture verses. This was a practice we had for years at home just before bedtime.*

I can recall those evenings with a great deal of warmth. Glad we had those times together. As a parent with the years fleeting by, children growing up, establishing themselves in this world of ours, I'm grateful for some of those good positive memories. I trust they will never go away.

The day before Alan was to leave, several of us were together in the den. He was sitting on the floor propped up against the sofa. I sat down beside him. Honestly, I was so aware that he was nineteen years old. The next day, he was going away for Marine basic training. I could feel it in my heart; life at home would never be quite the same again. Another one of our dear children would be leaving home. For me, there was pain in that awareness.

His room would no longer be a mess. Clean it up. It stays clean now. When I walk by it now, I realize it's the same as it was the day before. Momentarily, one wishes for a return of socks on the floor, a bed not made, shoes scattered here and there, and papers everywhere.

It's clean now. A boy has grown up into a man. Parents who are there or have been there know the tearing of the heart when this happens.

Where did all the years go? How did the time pass so fast? Life raises those questions. But it doesn't answer them. There's a certain mystery. I think it must remain there to demand an ever-flowing faith! A certain dependency upon God! The One who created us. The One in control! The One who loves us and redeemed us! The One for us!

The day Alan was to leave, he was standing tall, walking toward the back door, a bit in a hurry. I walked up to him, put my arms around him, and gave him a strong hug. I could sense the strong feelings in my heart for him. Love, mingled with pain. It was the turning of another page in the book of life for Alan, for me, for our entire family. Things would never be the same again.

That's the way it is with the growth process. Life moves forward. Not backward. Can't stop it.

> Children, obey your parents in the Lord: for
> this is right. (Ephesians 6:1 KJV)

> And, ye fathers, provoke not your children
> to wrath: but bring them up in the nurture and
> admonition of the Lord. (Ephesians 6:1, 4 KJV)

Leave a Godly Inheritance

❧◉◉☙

I t was a sad and unbelievable way to die. In the hospital. With one leg literally decaying. Rotting. The odor was so bad that the hospital confined her to an entirely separate place. Distant as possible from the other patients. That was how my grandmother Wells died. The mother of my mother. The mother of five girls, in total. No sons.

Interestingly, I can only recall how Grandmother Wells looked. I have no memory of her talking much. A quiet person. For years, I mistakenly thought that she was of American Indian ancestry. Because to me, she looked like an Indian. Very brown skin. Facial features Indian-like. We visited her and Granddad Wells several times in Daisy, Georgia, near Claxton, the world-renowned fruitcake town.

Nevertheless, as indicated, my memories of her are few. Quiet.

Looked much like an Indian. Died a terrible death. Also, she and my grandfather, who died after she did, had very few earthly possessions. At his death, his total assets were $18,000. That was the inheritance they left to be divided into their five girls. You may not believe it, but I also know they fought over the $18,000.

One thing is for sure. We all will die. Some quietly, peacefully. Some not so. Some leave a lot of inheritance here on earth to be divided; some leave very little.

The most important issue of life is the spiritual inheritance we gain at death, not the material stuff we leave behind! Then there will be no dispute!

The apostle Paul said, "I have finished the race, and have been faithful. So a crown will be given me for pleasing the Lord" (2 Timothy 4:7–8 CEV).

Faith Is the Answer

Yesterday, December 22, 2020, Erica called me and talked rapidly with some element of enthusiasm and joy. She is our twenty-nine-year-old granddaughter, who is presently living with her father and his current wife, her stepmother, in Louisiana.

In the midst of the conversation, she asked, "Can a Catholic go to heaven?" She was actually referring to her stepmother's father, who was on the verge of death.

My answer to her question was, "Yes. Sure." *John 3:16* applies to everyone. "*For God so loved the world that He gave His only begotten Son that whosoever believeth in Him should not perish but have everlasting life*" (KJV). Catholics, Baptists, Methodists, Presbyterians, Church of God, or whoever.

The word *believe*s in the original language is a present indicative active participle. That means that *the belief, the faith, is to be* continuous. *It's not a one-time moment or event. It's the beginning of, and an ongoing, for life, faith relationship with Jesus Christ as one's Savior and Lord. Similar to a marriage relationship. Commitment is involved and genuine faith!*

Reading the Bible daily helps you to keep on believing in Jesus Christ and will assure you of heaven!

> I know whom I have believed and am persuaded that He is able to keep that which I have committed unto Him against that day. (2 Timothy 1:12 KJV)

Hopefully You Can Recall Playful Memories

⋐⊙⊙⋑

My brother, Larry, and I were just a few months apart in age. He was born in September of 1936 and I in June of 1935. So we were close growing up, participating together in a lot of things. Going to church. Going to school. Sleeping together in a double bed. And getting into mischief and playing pranks often at the expense of others.

Somehow, I don't recall how we came to possess a guitar. Neither of us could play the thing, but we could strum it. Pick it.

Anyway, my mother had this young lady helping her at home. I think it might have been immediately after the birth of one of our sisters. I hid Larry in one of our large closets with the guitar and a white sheet covering him and the guitar.

I told Larry to sit quietly there. I then told him that I would ask the young lady helping Mom to go into the closet for some item. "When you hear her, strum on the guitar!" He did. The lady was so frightened by the surprising sound coming from under the sheet, not knowing it was Larry who was doing it. She ran out of the house, fearfully fleeing! We almost never got her to come back into the house.

Thought. I hope you have some playful, funny memories of your childhood. Hopefully, not always at the expense of others. I'm glad to have had a brother like Larry to grow up with.

> Rejoice in the Lord always, and again I say, Rejoice. (Philippians 4:4 KJV)

> A merry hear doeth good like a medicine. (Proverbs 17:22 KJV)

Read and Reread Romans, Chapter Eight

I was sitting in church one Sunday, listening to a special speaker who happened to be a famous scientist and a very strong Christian. This was sometime in 2019 as I recall.

He was very interesting, and two things that I recall that he said were the lack of Bible reading even among churchgoing people. Then he said that the most popular and favorite chapter in the Bible is now Romans chapter 8. I was surprised because I had always thought that Psalm 23 was the favorite.

Nevertheless, I strongly encourage you to read, study, and reread Romans 8. Whether it is the favorite or most popular chapter or not, it has been a powerful and extremely helpful scripture to me personally for years.

I have repeated verse 28 to myself many, many times. I encourage you to memorize that verse and meditate on it often.

> And we know that all things work together for good to them that love God, to them who are the called according to His purpose. (Romans 8:28 KJV)

Realize How Patient God and People Have Been with You

❧◉◉❧

It happened when I was in my senior year at Mercer University. I was still single and pastoring Middle Ground Baptist Church, near Eastman, Georgia.

Every Sunday night after church, I would drive back to Macon, many times falling asleep at the wheel. Then suddenly, I would be awakened when my front-right tire ventured off the pavement.

One Sunday morning, I preached a sermon on tithing. Warning everyone with great drama, "If you don't tithe the tenth, God may take it from you with flat tires or some other unexpected mishap." Then I left the pulpit to find I had not one but two flat tires on my forty-nine, two-door, black Chevrolet, waiting for me in the church parking area. I never used that illustration again when preaching on tithing or giving.

Admittedly, I was still young in 1956–1957, only twenty-one. Single. Very much green behind the ears as old-timers would say. Still learning. With lots to learn.

Thought. I look back, especially to my youth, and am reminded how patient God and many others have been with me. Hopefully, I'm still learning.

> Tell the Lord how thankful you are because
> He is kind and always merciful. (Psalm 118:29
> CEV)

Visualize Calming Places

❧❧❧

O ne of the things I love to do is visualize places I have been. See them clearly in my mind. Like flashing the pictures of those places on the screen of my mind.

One of the most calming and pleasant places we ever lived was Crisfield, Maryland (1969–1972). The people there on the Eastern Shore of Maryland were so loving, kind, and accepting of us, our whole family. They were humble and ordinary folk, but very special. I don't recall any arrogance in any of them.

They made it clear that they loved us individually. Wayne, Alan, Dianne, Linda, Gayle, and myself. And they loved us as a family.

It's a mind-calming, meditating experience for me to visualize the main street of Crisfield. The street that dead-ends right up to the Chesapeake Bay. The water. The gentle waves. The breeze. The beautiful sunny days. All together visualized, so calming.

Thought. For you, it may be sitting quietly on the ocean beach alone or with family and friends. Or it may be some other calming place. Recall it. Visualize it. It can calm your mind.

Be still, and know that I am God. (Psalm 46:1 KJV)

You Alone Must
Decide

⁕

Freedom, I've said many times before, is a wonderful and terrible thing. Can be either one. It all began in the Garden of Eden as described in the first few chapters of the Bible with Adam and Eve and God. God provided them with a paradise. Blessed beyond human imagination. Then God just warned them with one *don't*. It's the tree of life or death! If you eat of that tree, "You'll die." They had everything they needed.

But then God gave them one more thing. *Freedom to choose.*

Why would anyone choose the way of death rather than life? It means failure and foolishness. Like Adam and Eve. Good or bad. Failure or success. Why would anyone choose to fail when *the road to success is clearly mapped out in the Bible? Detailed simply in Psalm 1.*

Lesson point: Read carefully Psalm 1! Read it daily for thirty days. Memorize it. It tells you how to be successful! Also, read Proverbs. Read the chapter every day according to the day of the month. On the first day of the month, read carefully chapter 1 and so on.

Sin and self-satisfaction bring destruction and death to stupid fools. (Proverbs 1:32 CEV)

All wisdom comes from the Lord and so do common sense and understanding. (Proverbs 2:6 CEV)

Recall Peaceful and Serene Memories

૱૭૭

One night when we lived in Pennsylvania, in the late 1960s, we were visiting one of our church members who lived out in the country in a large farmhouse. It was in the middle of winter. It was a time of a full moon, and it was snowing. We were sitting inside at a place so located that we could watch the snowflakes softly falling on the rolling hills in the moonlight. A beautiful, serene, picturesque sight. So peaceful, calming to watch. We gazed out the window taking it all in.

Experiencing the snow was one of the new things that living in Pennsylvania gave us. It was a delightful gift never before enjoyed, having grown up in South Georgia.

For some reason, that particular night I mentioned above stands out in my memory. Perhaps it was early in our newly located home there. Having moved from New Orleans. No snow in New Orleans.

Thought. God gives us different things to calm our troubled minds. Sometimes, it may be softly falling snow in a moonlight night or even the memory of it.

> As soon as God speaks, the earth obeys. He covers the ground with snow like a blanket of wool. (Psalm 147:15–16 CEV)

> Peace I leave with you; my peace I give to you; not as the world gives do I give to you. Let not your heart be troubled, neither let them be afraid. (John 14:27 KJV)

Learn to Swim in
the River of Life

❧❧❧

O ne of the things my brother Larry and I often did in the summertime as teenagers was to swim upstream and downstream
in the Ocmulgee River near our hometown in Abbeville, Georgia.
The current was strong and swift in some of the places. And there
were the snakes and alligators that we were unaware of with our limited wisdom and common sense as a youth. We were never bitten by
a snake or alligator. Nevertheless, the dangers were there.

Life is somewhat like that. Some of life is like swimming downstream. But much of it is like swimming upstream. Strong and swift
current. Dangers whether we are aware or not.

*Reading the Bible and especially Proverbs will not keep the snakes,
the alligators, and swift currents out of the River of Life. But it will definitely help you to have the wisdom and common sense to successfully deal
with them and to stay alive.*

Wisdom makes life pleasant and leads us
safely along. (Proverbs 3:17 CEV)

Remember Your Source
of Blessings

ᴄᴓᴓᴖ

One thing that I have learned about squirrels is that they have a good memory. They don't forget easily. In fact, daily they obviously can remember where to find food.

Since being retired and having no schedule to be bound to, I have found pleasure in relatively small, simple things like reading, writing, and innocent chores. One of these chores that I do almost daily with pleasure is feeding the squirrels in my backyard. Often, I may see as many four, six, or eight at the same time.

Mind you, there is no sign in my backyard that reads "Squirrels come here for food." I do not ring a bell for them to come eat. I do not call them. I do not have to remind them in any way where and when the food is available. The pecans. The peanuts. The bread. The grapes. The apple peelings. The corn. Daily. They just remember. Very smart for wild little creatures. I enjoy watching them. One of the simple pleasures in my older, retired years.

The point for us to learn is that it is important for us to *remember the source of all we have*. Our food. Our shelter. Air we breathe. Life itself. Available eternal life if we believe.

> Then beware lest thou forget the Lord, which brought thee forth out of the land of Egypt, from the house of bondage. (Deuteronomy 6:12 KJV)

> Every good and perfect gift comes down from the Father who created all the lights in the heavens. (James 1:17 CEV)

Add a Touch of Humor

※ ◎ ※

Dianne is our second daughter and our second child. Born in New Orleans while I was a student in seminary there. Now she is a registered nurse, living nearby.

It was Sunday, and she called. "Have you all been out yet?" The question was relevant because of the COVID-19 virus that has kept us secluded for months away from large gatherings.

My response wasn't what she was asking for when I said, "Yes, I've gotten out of bed. I've fed the squirrels and have gone out to get the newspaper."

She laughed in response to my intended humor. She is quick-witted and a humorous person herself. She laughs easily with or at her husband and others.

Nevertheless, Dianne, since her early childhood and even infancy, has been independent-minded, feisty, and humorous in personality. Not bad qualities to possess. Her own three daughters also have similar qualities.

Point. For any person to meet life effectively and successfully, it's important to have a touch of humor. Being too serious, with no flexibility that laughter gives life, can break you or make you hard to live with.

> A merry heart maketh a cheerful countenance: but by sorrow of the heart the spirit is broken. (Proverbs 15:13 KJV)

> Always be glad because of the Lord! I will say again; Be glad. Always be gentle with others. (Philippians 4:4–5 CEV)

Start Young

February 2, 2021

I received an interesting phone call this afternoon from Dora and Byron Harbin, who reside in an assisted living facility in Hattiesburg, Mississippi. Byron is eighty-seven years old. Dora, his wife, is eighty-four. I have known Byron for over sixty years. I can honestly say that he has been a dear friend for all those years, since 1953.

We met in college at Norman Park, Georgia. From there, we followed each other on to Mercer University in Macon, Georgia, and then on to New Orleans Baptist Theological Seminary.

Byron, just a couple of years older than me, has always been a sincere Christian. After seminary years, he taught in a Baptist college in South Carolina. From there, he spent thirty years as a Southern Baptist Foreign Missionary in Brazil.

Now retired, like myself, he still expresses his appreciation for our longtime friendship. He is not well! Has suffered recently the deadly COVID virus. Before that were two open-heart surgeries. One in Brazil. One in the United States.

Though his voice is now very soft and measured, his spirit is still vibrant and positive!

The reason Byron is who he is and how he is today is that of who he was and how he was in his youth. His early years were a strong foundation for the remainder of his life.

> Keep your Creator in mind while you are young! In years to come, you will be burdened down with troubles and say, I don't enjoy life anymore. (Ecclesiastes 12:1 CEV)

Use Your Eyes to Look Up

Ellie, a large brown Lab, is Rick, my son-in-law, and daughter Linda's dog. A few days ago, they took Ellie to the vet's office for day surgery to have her other eye taken out. Now, both of her eyes are literally gone forever. She was already blind before her eyes had to be removed.

Interestingly, Rick stated that dogs handle blindness better than humans because, as he said, they have other senses to use. More senses. Better senses, like the smell and the like than we do.

Rick should know because he spends so much time observing and caring for Ellie. He pets her, talks to her, takes her for walks daily. Has spent thousands of dollars for the best of her care. Even cooks special chicken for her. I've never known anyone to take better care of their pets than Rick and Linda. They would not even think of "putting Ellie down" just because she's blind. To say they love their animal is a gross understatement!

Point. It's possible to have eyes, but still not see. It's also possible to have eyes but use them wrongly. Looking down, or to the left or right, horizontally, rather than up. *The Bible warns and instructs us!*

> Good people are kind to their animals. (Proverbs 12:10 CEV)

> Hear now this, O foolish people, and without understanding; which have eyes, and see not; which have ears, and hear not. (Jeremiah 5:21 KJV)

> I will lift up mine eyes unto the hills, from whence cometh my help. My help cometh from the Lord, which made heaven and earth. (Psalm 121:1 KJV)

Make Christ Your Purpose

I t was a Sunday morning at eleven in 2021. Gayle, my wife, and I were seated together in our den. Not in church for the past several months because of the COVID-19 virus scare all over the world. But we wanted to attend a Christian worship service as we have done since our childhood. Thus, this was very unusual, almost strange for us not to be attending a church, worshipping collectively with our friends. Not the way that had been a custom for us all our lives.

Now in our eighties at home on a Sunday morning. So out of character for us. But we could watch and listen to Christian songs and hear a sermon by way of television.

Today's sermon was based on Philippians 1:21 (KJV). "For me to live is Christ, and to die is gain." Simply delivered but very powerful and heartfelt. The Holy Spirit's work could be felt from the messenger. We certainly felt like we had heard a message from God. Encouraging and challenging. It was the apostle Paul's goal and purpose *"to live for Christ." It was his faith and hope. To die was to be with Christ.*

Point. Two extremely important facts. One is a challenge "to live for Christ." Make Him your purpose. The second is the realization that death for the Christian believer is a gain, not a loss.

> But seek first His Kingdom and His righteousness and all these things shall be yours as well. (Matthew 6:33 RSV)

> Precious in the sight of the Lord is the death of His Saints. (Psalm 116:15 KJV)

Seek Wisdom for Decisions

꩜

Decisions are something that is a must. We can't avoid decisions from the time we put our feet on the floor in the morning until the time we put our feet back in the bed at night.

Example. There I was in Publix. Deciding, "Do I need to pick up more bananas?" Then I must decide how many bananas. Two? Three?

Five? Do I get ripe ones? Green ones? Which? If I get too many too ripe, they will rot before we eat them.

Another example. I looked at a used car, a 2011 model. At first glance, I decided I liked it. Later, I drove it. Decided I didn't like it. Quick decision. That decision, while seemingly larger, is more important than the bananas. I made it faster than the one regarding the bananas.

Why do some small decisions often seem so difficult and the larger ones easier? I don't know! The banana decision seemed at the time to have more parts. The car deal was seemingly simple. I just didn't like it. Didn't feel good. How we make decisions will determine our lives. *Our own and often many others. For the now. And for the next generation. Our family. Our friends. Others.*

Many decisions, especially large ones, I pray about. It often feels that I'm alone in the final moment. *That's why reading the Bible is important. It does teach us common sense and wisdom.*

With wisdom you will learn what is right
and honest and fair. (Proverbs 2:9 CEV)

Stay Alert to Life's Changes

〰️

A few days ago, I was driving from Baltimore to Norfolk under and over the Chesapeake Bay between Maryland and Virginia's Eastern Shore. The Chesapeake area is an interesting area. Country, fields, and salt waters altogether. Seagulls. Crabs and Oysters. My family and I lived there from 1967 to 1972. Our four children were still young. It was what I often refer to as our wonder years. Kids at home every day and night. Always knew where they were and what they were doing. Peaceful.

Nevertheless, if you know the Chesapeake Bay Bridge-Tunnel, you know, as you cross the Bay there, sometimes you are under the bay and sometime over the bay. It demands being an alert driver. Heavy traffic. Narrow lanes. The possibility of an accident is very real. No time to be distracted. A bit dangerous to say the least.

Thought. Life is a lot like the Chesapeake Bay Bridge-Tunnel.

Sometimes we feel on top of it. Other times under it. *Life doesn't stay still and quiet, easy, with the kids all home safely tucked in. Life rises and falls, up and under.* Can be dangerous at times. Heavy traffic issues. Must stay physically, mentally, and spiritually alert.

Reading the Bible daily, especially Proverbs and Psalm 1, helps to keep us alert.

> And that, knowing the time, that now it is high time to awake out of sleep: for now is our salvation nearer than when we believed. (Romans 13:11 KJV)

Pray for Positive,
Healthy Thoughts

This is a personal confession. Sometimes I wrestle with my own thoughts. I get frustrated with them. Often, they have to do with circumstances or persons over which I have no control. Nevertheless, the thoughts belong to me. My personal possessions. Not calm and still. They bounce around in my head like a ping-pong ball back and forth. Uncontrolled. The thoughts may be in the form of frustration. Anxiety. Worry. Fear. Regret. Grief. Or sadness.

So whatever I name them, they are negative. Not good. Like garbage in my mind. So what do I do with the garbage in my mind? Where and how do I get rid of my mind of garbage? It's not easy. It takes work.

One thing I do is pray for my thoughts, "God, help me to have good, positive, healthy thoughts. Please cleanse my mind of the garbage." Reading, meditating on the Bible, helps. Then I may even talk to someone, a friend, or maybe my wife.

Jesus said

> I tell you not to worry about your life. (Matthew 6:25 CEV)

> Cast thy burden upon the Lord, and He shall sustain thee. He shall never suffer the righteous to be moved. (Psalm 55:22 KJV)

> Thou wilt keep him in perfect peace, whose mind is stayed on Thee; because he trusteth in Thee. (Isaiah 26:3 KJV)

Tame and Control Your Mind

ﾟ

One of the things I enjoy doing in my senior years is watching old western movies. And it's interesting to watch the cowboys of yesteryears tame wild horses.

From the wild, they tame the horses to be useful, very serviceable, horses pulling buggies and being ridden by the cowboys.

Reminds me of one of the greatest needs of man. That is to tame his mind. Like the horses, it is not easy to tame.

Another word to use is *control*. The mind can be like a wild horse. It can be dangerously out of control.

It's left up to each individual to "tame" and "control" his own mind. And that can only be done with God's help.

There is the human tendency, innately in each human, from early life to later years, for the mind to go astray, jump the fences, wildly out of control.

Only with God's help can anyone tame and control his mind. And it's a matter of life or death. A matter of peace. Or mental, physical, and spiritual chaos.

> Everyone who is ruled by the Holy Spirit thinks about spiritual things. If our minds are ruled by our desires, we will die. If our minds are ruled by the Spirit, we will have life and peace. (Romans 8:5–6 CEV)

Be a Man of
God, Learning

⟋⟍⟋⟍⟋

"*L et us be men! Men of God! Men of God, learning!*" That was a sermon I heard in New Orleans at the Baptist Theological Seminary Chapel where I was a student in 1959–1962, earning my master of divinity degree. I heard many sermons in the chapel while living on campus.

I'm sure many of the sermons and lectures influenced my thinking, but that's the only one I vividly remember.

Actually, that one would be enough to meet the responsibilities of life. *Be a man! Be a man of God! Be a man of God, learning!*

What does it mean to take and shoulder the responsibilities of being a man? It takes a sense of dependency on God to enable a man to be a man. Because it's impossible to truly, honestly, and genuinely shoulder that burden without God's help. Then, even with God's help, it takes a strong and open mind to keep learning how to do that as each man faces the ever-changing weight of that responsibility.

> Everyone with good sense wants to learn.
> (Proverbs 18:15 CEV)

> Blessed is the man that walketh not in the counsel of the ungodly, no standeth in the way of sinners, nor sitteth in the seat of the scornful. But his delight is in the law of the Lord; and in his law doth he meditate day and night. (Psalm 1:1–2 KJV)

Remember that Wisdom and
Success Come from God

⋲⟨ৎ⟩⟨ৎ⟩⋺

When we moved from New Orleans to Pennsylvania in 1962, the goal was to build a church from birth. This means that they had no building and no land, only a few people from the South who wanted a Southern Baptist Church in Carlisle. However, those Southerners, shortly after we arrived, moved away. Some went back South. We were left with only a few native Pennsylvanians, which turned out to be just fine.

In essence, God gave us exactly what we needed. Sort of like a Gideon group. Smaller but adequate. We bought two acres of land in a beautiful setting. Built a nice building. And grew to over a hundred in attendance by 1967.

So what might have seemed like threatening failure turned out to be doing it God's way obviously because of God's intervention. His provision.

It was a great experience for us, a young couple from the South, getting to know some wonderful people in a different place and culture.

Probably many lessons I was taught but mainly one. Don't be too quick to diagnose your situation. What might seem like a downward turn might be God's way of setting up your situation to teach you that it was not by your own strength but God's.

> For with God nothing shall be impossible.
> (Luke 1:37 KJV)

> As the Apostle Paul said, "I have planted, Apollos watered; but God gave the increase. (1 Corinthians 3:6 KJV)

In Spite of Tears, Think about the Future

❦

The other night, I was on the phone with my younger sister, Kay. We were talking about our younger brother, Tony. Kay is a registered nurse. Tony is retired, and although the youngest of all five of our siblings, he currently is in very bad health. While he has survived cancer of the throat and just recently had internal bleeding in his kidneys, blood pooled in his abdomen. What next?

Anyway, Kay and I were talking seriously about Tony. Then, almost out of the blue, I choked up and was not able to say another word. I was slowly able to say, "Do you ever wish you could talk to Mom and Dad about things? Do you miss them?" Tears were present with me, I admit. Maybe you'd think a grown-up man in years, not a small child, would confess to still missing the presence and availability of his parents. He ought to be more grown-up, more mature, more independent. I'm not. I still feel their absence, especially when their youngest child, our youngest brother, seemed to be facing immediate and certain death. And nothing we could do about it!

I may never reach the place to be totally independent of the need for family and friends. And certainly, never become independent of my need for God's encouragement, helping hand, and His willingness to listen to my prayers. *Just the way it is. Life here and now! But the good news is in the future!*

> Yes, God will make His home among His people. He will wipe all tears from their eyes, and there will be no more death, suffering, crying, or pain. These things of the past are gone forever. (Revelation 21:3–4 CEV)

Have an Anchor for Your Soul

A few months ago, I rode through downtown Abbeville, Georgia. It was so drastically different from what I remembered it to be when I lived there in my youth. I grew up there from age five to eighteen when I finished Abbeville High School. Eighteen in the graduating class.

But Abbeville downtown wasn't there when I rode through recently. No people were on the streets. The stores were all closed, boarded up. The theater. The barbershop. The two drugstores where you could buy two dips of ice cream for a dime and a banana split for thirty-five cents. All the grocery stores, seven of them, where you could buy six cokes for a quarter and lots of penny candy back in the early 1950s. Not so today. Neither does my old school exist today. I walked through the empty hallways. Empty classrooms. So quiet. No chatter of kids. No rushing here and there. No teachers. No principal's office.

Change was everywhere. Silence. No vibrant life. Stillness. A sense of meaninglessness everywhere. You could see it and feel it.

Abbeville, like lots of small towns, has changed. Many no longer even exist. Never witnessed the slow process of change, but it is so evident now. Admittedly, there is a bit of sadness in the realization. So many things are not here anymore. Just not the same. However, *it's encouraging to know some things never change!*

> Jesus Christ the same yesterday, and today,
> and forever. (Hebrews 13:8 KJV)

> This hope is like a firm and steady anchor
> for our souls. (Hebrews 6:19 CEV)

Pray with Persistence and Patience

⸎

There I was on an oil rig out in the middle of the Gulf waters, fishing, near Buras, Louisiana, in 1961. At that time, we lived in Buras for the summer. All three of us, Gayle, myself, and our daughter, Linda Gayle, age two.

The fishing event was at night. There were lights on the oil rig. Bugs of all kinds were attracted to the bright bulbs. When these insects and flies touched the hot lights, it meant their death and sudden fall into the bay waters.

That was where we were fishing. Near the oil rig where the insects were falling. The fish were swimming right on top of the water catching the falling insects.

It was my kind of fishing! No sitting and waiting. Just simply dropping my line in the water and immediately pulling up a fish.

Thought. I've compared that fishing experience to my prayer life. My desire, admittedly, is for God to answer my prayers that way. Immediately. But most of the time, not so! Sometimes, if not often, my prayers have been answered after years of waiting. *Prayer demands persistence and patience.*

> I patiently waited, Lord, for You to hear my prayer. You listened and pulled me from a lonely pit. (Psalm 40:1 CEV)

> Wait on the Lord and keep His way. (Psalm 37:34 KJV)

Handle Children Carefully

❧⟨◉⟩❧

We were in the Baptist Hospital in New Orleans on August 18, 1959. Gayle had just given birth to Linda Gayle, our first child. I was seated in another room waiting for her to come out of the labor and delivery room.

Suddenly, I saw not my wife but a little red-headed figure being brought for me to see, weighing less than six pounds. The part of her entry that so caught my attention was the red hair. She had lots of hair at birth. I don't have red hair. Gayle doesn't. However, it does run in the bloodlines of both of us. My grandfather and her uncle.

Gayle was twenty-two. I was twenty-four. There we were away from our home state of Georgia. Our firstborn child was born in a different city and a different state. Away from our family and friends. Actually, in a different culture.

Two things I vividly remember, the red hair and how fragile our new baby was. When arriving back to our apartment hours later, getting out of the car, Gayle said to me, "Here, take Linda while I get out of the car." I was fearful as a young father to hold a very young baby girl.

Thought. How we care for children is extremely important!

> Children are a blessing and a gift from the Lord. (Psalm 127:3 CEV)

> Parents, don't be hard on your children. Raise them properly. Teach them and instruct them about the Lord. (Ephesians 6:4 CEV)

Be Thankful for Good Parents

Just thinking out loud on a quiet Saturday morning. Recalling how good my Sovereign God has been to me. Places He has led me as *my Shepherd.* People He has permitted me to be friends with. Young and old. Rich and poor. Educated and uneducated. White-collar and blue-collar.

Thinking of where I came from. Not from wealth. Dad was a sharecropper in those early years in Rhine, Georgia, where I was born in 1935. Not known for a prosperous era. Great Depression times. I recall the dirt streets in Rhine. Pigs roamed the unattended streets in the middle of town.

One of my uncles was shot and killed in Rhine. My aunt Edna's verbal response when learning of her husband's death was, "Well, he won't hurt me anymore."

Also, my grandfather who lived near Rhine was known to strike fear in his own family as a drinking man with a bad reputation. He too could be dangerous with a gun.

But my father and mother turned the tide for me. They gave me a Christian home. Discipline, hard work, *reading the Bible,* and attending church were vital parts of my growing-up years. *I have so much to be grateful for, especially God-fearing parents.*

> Honor thy father and mother; which is the first commandment with promise; that it may be well with thee, and thou mayest live long on the earth. (Ephesians 6:2–3 KJV)

Honor Your Parents

Larry, my younger brother, was a risk-taking teenager only fourteen or so when this happened. He was at Poor Robin Springs, about a mile or two from Abbeville, Georgia, where we lived. The only way we got to Poor Robin Springs was to walk or ride our bikes. Anyway, we often went there with other teens to go swimming in the hot summertime.

On that particular day, Larry was there, not dressed in a swimming suit. He was fully dressed in clothes, shoes, and socks. Someone bet him $2 that he would not jump into the icy cold spring with his clothes on. Not knowing, I guess, that my young brother was easy to take a risk, especially when $2 was involved. A lot of money for either of us in the early 1950s.

The *bet* words were hardly out of the guy's mouth when Larry ran and jumped into the cold spring, clothes, shoes, and all.

Later when Dad heard about it, he made Larry give the $2 to the church offering. Reason said. Not to be betting whether we agreed or not.

That's the way it was in our homelife in the early 1950s. Dad pretty much called the shots. We followed the rules. Obeyed our parents for the most part. Dad was in charge. It was not a democracy at our house. Somehow, I think that was best. Like it or not. Dad was wiser.

> Honor thy father and thy mother: that thy
> days may be long upon the land which the Lord
> thy God giveth thee. (Exodus 20:12 KJV)

Ask God for an Excellent Mate

S he was smiling, having been awakened by me standing by her bedside. Really, she had not been asleep; she just acted like she was being awakened from her afternoon nap. Then she was laughing as I was handing her a birthday card. It just happened to be her eighty-fourth birthday. Eighty-four years and she has lived with me for sixty-three of them. She has been my partner, my lover, the mother of our four children. Two girls. Two boys.

From the four of them, there are eight grandchildren and three great-grandchildren.

She has followed me from state to state. First from Georgia to New Orleans, to Pennsylvania. Finally, to Maryland, then back to Georgia after twenty-three years traveling from our home base.

She has been not just a good wife and mother, grandmother, and great-grandmother but par excellence. All her children, grandchildren, daughters-in-law, and sons-in-law praise her that way. The best any of them or myself could ask or hope for.

I'm fully aware that not every man can speak of his wife that way. Not honestly, but it's true with me. A fact. None of our family disagrees. All the needed evidence is there.

She is a very unusual person, a special woman. Her family is at the very center of her being. Her heart. And we all know it.

> She takes good care of her family and is never lazy. Her children praise her, and with great pride her husband says, There are many good women, but you are the best. (Proverbs 31:27–29 CEV)

Accept Your Differences
and Be Thankful

಄ೕ಄ೂ

It was a recent Saturday. Gayle was on me about a haircut. She is always concerned about how my hair looks. I'm not Samson with strength in my hair length, but I usually like my hair longer than she does. Why? I don't know. Just one of those things. Our differences. She also likes her own hair short.

After my haircut, I met her at Publix for some grocery shopping together. We can agree on buying groceries together. Usually, because I leave that up to her. She knows best. Maybe I don't want to make those decisions. Food. Meals.

Funny how males and females, like the two of us, are so different. Yet we need each other. In fact, I know that I'm dependent on her for many things. Like it or not. Different or not. That is true. I admit it!

There is that mystery between the sexes. Husbands and wives. People, even generations, keep searching. Keep marrying and divorcing. Marrying again. Seeking. Like a hidden treasure. One man once told me, in his fourth marriage, "I wish I had just stayed with my first wife." Some things are illusive.

Some problems and questions have no clear-cut answers. That's just the way it is. Accept it. Don't waste good time searching for hidden treasures at the end of some mysterious rainbow.

> Who findeth a wife findeth a good thing,
> and obtaineth favor of the Lord. (Proverbs 18:22
> KJV)

Two Are Better than One

The two of us were sitting quietly together in her car eating ice-cream cones. The same kind we often buy at Brewsters. She got a waffle cone with butter pecan ice cream. I ordered the same. It was a beautiful afternoon. The cost of both treats together was over $10. We talked of remembering our teenage years when you could buy double dips for ten cents. A nickel per dip at the local corner drugstore in the 1950s.

We're not teenagers now. Over seventy years have flashed by. Years ago, we used to park together just to be together as college students. Meaningful moments. There on this Sunday afternoon with cones in hand, sometimes we conversed. Other times, we just sat quietly, watching cars speed by or people just gathering for ice-cream cones with their families.

The one thing I reminded myself of is two together are better than one. Often three is a crowd, but two together with ice-cream cones and wonderful memories together make a valuable, meaningful moment, *especially if the other person is your wife and friend.*

> Two are better than one, because they have a
> good reward for their toil. For if they fall one will
> lift up his fellow; but woe to him who is alone
> when he falls and has not another to lift him up.
> (Ecclesiastes 4:9–10 RSV)

Listen and Don't Be Quick to Judge

A t the age of eighty-five, there I was driving alone lost in Norfolk, Virginia. I had just successfully made it through the twenty-mile Bay Bridge-Tunnel, crossing the Chesapeake Bay between the Eastern Shore of Maryland and Virginia.

But that success was of no good to me at that moment because I couldn't find my way out of Norfolk. I had already asked two people for directions to Interstate 95. Still lost but not frustrated. I decided to stop again. And ask again.

So there I was asking this seemingly awkward, middle-aged man, "Can you tell me how to get to Interstate 95?"

Quickly, I was made aware of his inability to speak clearly. He stuttered. His face, his neck, and his head jerked back and forth involuntarily. Earnestly trying to answer my question. He knew the answer but stumbled with his speech impediment. He finally got these words out, "I'll write it down for you." And he did. With three well-written lines. *They were correct. I thanked him and was on my way easily. He had helped me find my way.*

Thought. It's a wise moment when we take time to listen. Outward appearances may not tell the whole story of a person. They may be wiser than we first think.

> My friends, if you have faith in our glorious Lord Jesus Christ you won't treat some people better than others. (James 2:1 CEV)

> We worship you Lord… You said to me, "I will point out the road that you should follow." (Psalm 32:6, 8 CEV)

Realize Your Bad Circumstances
May Become a Blessing

ᏋᎧᏋᏦᏋ

Your bad circumstances may become a blessing. Don't think your bad current circumstances are the end of the road for you. They may be the beginning of blessings that are hidden in your eyes at the moment.

Consider Joseph's story in the Bible recorded in Genesis and mentioned in Psalm. Envied and hated by his own brothers and sold into slavery in Egypt. His brothers lied to their father. Told him that Joseph had been killed. Jacob, the father, grieved greatly.

God used all those circumstances to lead Joseph to become one of the highest-ranking officials in Egypt.

Personally, I have experienced bad circumstances that turned out to be great blessings. Left a job in 1982 that I loved. Then lost a job in 1988. Those circumstances that felt like the end of the road were the beginning of a new and better road. Even to this day, I am reaping the rewards of those seemingly bad circumstances in 1982 and 1988.

Thought. Regardless of your circumstances, don't ever think God has forgotten you. He has not left you alone. Have faith and pray!

> Joseph remained a slave until his own words had come true, and the Lord had finished testing him. Then the King of Egypt set Joseph free and put him in charge of everything he owned. (Psalm 105:19–21 CEV)

> And we know that all things work together for good to them that love God, to them who are

called according to his purpose. (Romans 8:28 KJV)

You were in serious trouble, but you prayed to the Lord, and He rescued you. (Psalm 107:6 CEV)

Give Cheerfully with Love

◈◈◈

Our son, Wayne, doesn't live on a farm as my grandparents did with nine hundred acres of land, mules, cows, and chickens in South Georgia. But he does live on five acres of land with a dog, rabbits, a cat, and chickens. Once he also had a goat. All this in North Georgia.

So when he recently came to visit us, his mother and me, he brought a dozen eggs, the product of his chickens. Fresh eggs. Very big eggs.

They were different in size and likely fresh. Tasted about the same as store-bought.

But the main difference was, they were a gift from our own son. He delivered them personally. He raised the chickens. He feeds them daily with the help of his little Emma, our granddaughter. So all of that information being true made the eggs very special. A personal, caring gift from family, loved ones, I can even picture in my mind Emma caring for the hens. Using her little hands. Throwing grain on the ground for the chickens.

Thought. Not all gifts are the same. Some may be small. But when they are personal and given with love, they are very special.

> Every man according as he purposeth in his heart, so let him give; not grudgingly, or of necessity: for God loveth a cheerful giver. (2 Corinthians 9:7 KJV)

> And whoever gives to one of these little ones even a cup of water because he is a disciple, truly, I say to you, he shall not lose his reward. (Matthew 10:42 RSV)

Let God Guide You for Your Own Well-Being

I t was a pitiful and scary sight. A small child running down the street with no supervision. No parent. No guardian. Alone. In the middle of a very busy street. Cars and trucks everywhere.

Everything appeared to be a normal busy morning in the active neighborhood. But a small child running loose, unattended, caught my attention. Not a good sight.

The situation: The child ignored the moving vehicles. Several cars slammed on brakes to avoid hitting the little three-foot-tall child.

So I ran after the child. Caught him. He started kicking, screaming. Wanted to be free to go his own aimless way. Several minutes later, his frantic and hysterical mother showed up. Her child, without her knowing, had snuck out of their home. Aimlessly running down a busy street. Could have been badly hurt. Without a guardian or parent.

Thought. An adult child told me yesterday that he didn't like being told what not to do. If, for example, he was told he should quit smoking, he would become rebellious and not quit.

How often are we adults like small kids? Running loose, away from a guardian. So unaware of the dangers of being away from a guardian. Unaware of the dangers of being without God's guidance.

Let God guide you. It's for your own well-being!

> I (God) will instruct thee and teach thee in
> the way which thou shalt go: *I* will guide thee
> with mine eye. (Psalm 32:8)

Realize Generational Patterns
Can Be Changed!

ഏ⊚ഌ

R hine, Georgia. 1937. As told to me by my parents.
I was eighteen months old and had diphtheria. My dad at the time was a poor sharecropper. He went to his father, my grandfather, a nine hundred-acre farmer with a request.

"Will you loan me money to buy medicine for my eighteen-month-old son, Warren, who has diphtheria?"

My grandfather's reply was, "Why are you wasting money on medicine? Why don't you save the money for his casket?"

That was my grandfather. His attitude. His honest thoughts. That's who he was. His reputation. His character.

Nevertheless, I lived anyway. Survived diphtheria. God had a purpose for my life. He kept me alive and has to this day.

My dad, while admittedly was also somewhat rough around the edges, decided to be a different man. Different from his father! My dad was an example that generational patterns can be changed! *IT IS YOUR DECISION!*

Reading the Bible daily will not make us perfect. BUT it will help us to change for the better, regardless of what our childhood was like.

> Blessed is the man that walketh not in the counsel of the ungodly, nor standeth in the way of sinners, nor sitteth in the seat of the scornful. But his delight is in the law of the Lord; and in his law doth he meditate day and night! (Psalm 1:1–2 KJV)

Know that You Can Overcome Failure

❦

"We don't need you anymore." In essence, that is what I was told by my employer. In so many, not so nice words, I was fired! That has happened to me twice in my lifetime. A long time ago!

If you live long enough *you will meet failure in some way.* Maybe at a job, or as a parent, or a marriage, or school, or something. No one makes a home run every time. Sometimes we don't even make it to first base. We all are human. Life is not always fair.

So, what do you do with failure? I can honestly tell you that reading the Bible daily, has every time helped me get back on my feet! Every time! Especially Psalm 1 and Proverbs. I believe it will help you too!

> The steps of a good man are ordered by the Lord; and He delights in his way.
> Though he fall, he shall not be utterly cast down; for the Lord upholds him with his hand.
> (Psalm 37:23–24 KJV)

Know There Is a Friend Who Will Never Leave You

༺ৡৢৡৢৡ༻

There I stood, alone, by James's graveside. He was my best friend all during elementary school, middle school, and high school in Abbeville, Georgia. The only time I remember us having a disagreement was in the third grade when we both liked the same little girl, Sara. She was cute with freckles and pigtails. But she moved away the next year, and that solved the only problem we ever had.

We visited each other's homes. Knew each other's parents. Went to basketball games together. Shared good values and morals.

Although he stayed in Georgia after high school, I lived in different states. But at several high school reunions, we were always glad to catch up with old times.

But not so anymore as I stood there at his graveside. He was born in 1934. I was born in 1935. It was on a sunny day, with good memories of a good friend, but admittedly with very somber feelings.

Thought. It's good to remind myself that Jesus is my friend. He will never die and leave me. It is my choice to make Him my Lord and friend. It's each person's choice to make Jesus Christ his or her Lord and friend. Reading the Bible daily helps us choose friends wisely.

You are my choice, and you keep me safe. You make my life pleasant, and my future is bright. I praise You, Lord, for being my guide. I will always look to You, as You stand beside me. (Psalm 16:5–8 CEV)

The Lord spake unto Moses face to face, as a man speaketh *unto his friend.* (Exodus 33:11 KJV)

When Facing Your Pharaoh,
Fear Not—Have Faith in God

ﾐﾐﾐﾐ

D o you remember the account in the Bible of Moses leading the
children of Israel out of Egypt? They had just left after years
of slavery in Egypt. However, Pharaoh, who had permitted them to
leave, suddenly changed his mind and was chasing after them with all
of his soldiers, horses, and chariots. Pharaoh had much more power
than the Israelites and was certainly capable of recapturing them and
returning them to slavery.

So there they were. Moses and the Israelites were helpless and
afraid. They were grumbling, complaining to Moses, and saying why
he didn't just leave them in Egypt in the first place.

They feared that they were about to die in the wilderness.

> Then, Moses said unto the people, "Fear
> ye not, stand still, and see the salvation of the
> Lord, which He will show to you today." (Exodus
> 14:13 KJV)

Thought. It may not be a truth easy to grasp, but it's there. *When
we may feel helpless facing our own Pharaoh, whatever it may be*, it's a
truth to think about.

> Cast your cares on the Lord and He will sus-
> tain you. (Psalm 55:22 KJV)

Self-Respect Is a
Day-by-Day Goal

∾⊙⊙⊱

O ne thing I do every day. Not out of conceit, just concern, how I look or feel. That is, I'm looking in the mirror at myself. Brushing my teeth. Combing my small amount of hair. Shaving.

But in the process of all that stuff we call personal hygiene, I'm looking at myself thinking, *I must face myself today. I must live with myself.*

Whom will I be? How will I live? What will I do? What will be my thoughts? My words. How will I spend this day? My time. Realizing every day I have less time left on this earth, my death is certain.

Self-respect is so important for all of us because we have to live with ourselves. Will I be thankful at the end of the day or regretful from the waste of time?

My prayer for myself includes at least three or four things. "Help me, Lord, this day to be what you want me to be with my thoughts, my words. My actions." Wrapping those together helps a day to be meaningful and worthwhile.

Thought. When we are able to face ourselves at the end of the day with no guilt or regrets, that's a day well spent.

This is the day which the Lord hath made; we
will rejoice and be glad in it. (Psalm 118:24 KJV)

Let the words of my mouth and the med-
ication of my heart be acceptable in Thy sight,
O Lord, my strength, and my redeemer. (Psalm
19:14 KJV)

Stay Alert to God's Care

⚮

This was 1956 when I was a college student at Mercer University. It often happened to me late on Sunday nights, driving alone back to Mercer in Macon, Georgia. I would fall asleep at the wheel of my forty-nine, two-door, black, Chevrolet. What kind of shape my tires were in, I don't know.

But as I drove along with no white line painted on the outside of the highway to help guide me, with sleepy eyes, my right front tire would fall off the edge of the black pavement. That jerk of the tire would always wake me up.

I would be tired with my sleepiness. Young, at the age of twenty-one, I was a pastor of a small country church near Eastman. I would have preached twice. Sunday morning and evening worship services.

It's amazing to me as I look back how frequently that Sunday night experience was that I never wrecked. That single jerk of the front tire falling off the edge of the black pavement would always awaken me.

> The Lord says, if you love me and truly know who I am, I will rescue you and keep you safe. (Psalm 91:14 CEV)

> The Lord is your protector, and He won't go to sleep or let you stumble. The protector of Israel doesn't doze or even get drowsy. (Psalm 121:3–4 CEV)

Learn to Live with
Your Scars

⋘⊙⊙⊙⊙⋙

O ftentimes, scars stay with us for a long time. We may mentally forget about them, then someone reminds us.

A recent visit to a medical doctor reminded me of something that happened to me when I was about twelve years old.

He asked me a simple question, "When did you get into a fight?" as he examined my nose. The inside of my nose has scars that indicated to his observation I had been injured in the past.

I responded that I had never been in such a fight. Then I remembered that when I was about twelve, I had run into another child face-first. Running fast, we met suddenly at the corner of my home. Coming from opposite directions. His forehead collided with my nose and mouth. I received stitches on my lip. Nothing said about my nose.

Nevertheless, the medical doctor recently informed me that there is scar evidence, which hinders my breathing. Since childhood, I have lived with physical scars on my nose.

Thought. Life happens to all of us. Accidents. Events in times and places. We may forget. But scars are often made that affect us. Some good. Some physical. Some emotional. *Learning to live with them is part of what life is about.*

The apostle Paul, who had many scars from life, said, "I have learned, in whatsoever state I am, therewith to be content" (Philippians 4:11 KJV).

> Christ gives me the strength to face any-
> thing. (Philippians 4:13 CEV)

Reading the Bible daily, especially Proverbs, teaches us how.

Consider All the Pieces in Making a Decision

❧❦❧

Oftentimes in life, a decision is like a puzzle. It has many pieces, small and large. Like a puzzle, there is not one sizeable reason for deciding something. To buy or to sell. To move or to stay.

One of the small pieces of the puzzle of my decision to move once had to do with the house we lived in. It was not the only reason, but it certainly influenced my decision. It was a big decision too. The decision to move from Maryland to Georgia in 1982.

We lived in a house that I never liked for ten years. I made myself live there. We had moved from a house in Crisfield, Maryland, that I loved to this house in Pasadena, Maryland. I remodeled the downstairs, put in a fireplace, and tried to fix it as I would like it. But I never did.

So never learning to like that house and having an opportunity to move to a nicer house in Georgia were not the reasons, but they're definitely pieces of the puzzle that influenced my decision.

Thought. Maybe it's a part of wisdom to examine different pieces of the puzzle one faces. Whatever the puzzle may be. A decision is often a puzzle with many parts. There are often small pieces that influence the final decision.

> If any of you need wisdom, you should ask
> God, and it will be given to you. God is generous
> and won't correct you for asking. But when you
> ask for something, you must have faith and not
> doubt. (James 1:5–6 CEV)

Stay Loving and Lovable, Especially to Loved Ones

⚜

We were standing in line in Tifton, Georgia, waiting for the next cashier to register our purchases when a friendly man came up behind us. In the conversation, we learned that he was a Baptist minister. He then, after we told him that we had been married for sixty-four years, told us that one of the things he informed young people in premarital counseling was, "She won't always look like this." And "He won't always look like he does now in his youth." In other words, youthful beauty fades away. Wrinkles occur.

The fact of the matter is, so many other things happen. We age. We struggle with life's inevitable issues. Children come on the scene. Often there are health problems. Financial problems.

Perhaps greatest of all, problems may be about relationships. Getting along with one another and others, even our own relatives, is not always easy. In fact, it may often be hard work!

Quitting and leaving may be easy.

It takes a lot of loving, forgetting, and forgiving to stay in a good relationship with almost anyone, including yourself and even loved ones.

> Love is kind and patient, never jealous, boastful, proud, or rude. Love isn't selfish or quick tempered. It doesn't keep a record of wrongs that others do. (1 Corinthians 13:4–5 CEV)

Reading the Bible daily, especially Proverbs, encourages and helps us to love our loved ones, even when they are not so lovable.

Realize Hard Work and Less May Be Better than Easy and More

∽◌◌◌◌∽

In the 1940s, Grandmother Burnham's woodburning cookstove was in the kitchen at the very end of the house. One purpose of the kitchen being at the end of the house was that in case it caught fire, hopefully, they could put the flame out before it burned the whole house down. Mind you, the kitchen was sparse. No refrigerator present. No running water. No electricity. Thus, no additional helpful appliances of any kind. No dishwasher. No toaster. Of course, no air conditioner. Not even a fan, unless it was one in your hand that you waved manually at your face.

So to say that it was a very hot room in the hot South Georgia summer was very much an understatement. It was small. Two or three people there made it crowded. So how did Grandmother cook three full meals a day? A hearty breakfast, including biscuits. Lunch. And supper. For her twelve children, herself, her husband, and sometimes extras for many years. Then lived to be ninety-seven years old. Outlived some of her own children. Amazing woman!

An extremely simple and hardworking lifestyle. And she was a woman of sincere faith in God and attended church on Sunday.

When I consider our country, our culture, our morals, our character today, comparing the 1940s to 2021, also keeping in mind that my grandmother's generation raised the "Greatest Generation," is hard work and tough better than less work and easy lifestyles?

> Wherefore I perceive that there is nothing better, than that a man should rejoice in his own works. (Ecclesiastes 3:22)

Look Up in Times
Like These

⟡

It was a Monday morning. Linda, our daughter, and Rick, her husband, were supposed to be at the hospital by 5:30 a.m. Linda's open-heart surgery was to be at 7:00 or 7:30 a.m. There would need to be about a two-hour preparation time.

Gayle and I had previously called many of our relatives and friends, requesting that they pray for the success of Linda's surgery. We were admittedly concerned, anxious at the thought of our first child, at her age of sixty-one, having such a serious and massive surgery.

The doctors had already told us that it would be a risky surgery. Not a good candidate. But the risk of not having the surgery would be even greater.

Our other three children, Dianne, Alan, and Wayne, called Linda on Sunday, reassuring her of their love, prayers, and encouragement.

Such concern and support from earthly loved ones are powerful and meaningful in such a time. Their support and verbal response were strengthening to us, their parents. We needed the horizontal help and the vertical help as we looked up to God with faith!

Thought. What do you do in times when you feel completely helpless? Absolutely nothing more you can do! You are one hundred percent dependent! You are tense and beyond words!

> I will lift up mine eyes unto the hills, from whence cometh my help. My help cometh from the Lord, which made heaven and earth. (Psalm 121:1–2 KJV)

Know that Reputation
Is Important

∽⊙⌒⊙∾

We were seated at our dining table in our kitchen. Just the two of us. Gayle and I. Eating. A peaceful moment. Then she exclaimed, almost a shout, "There's a snake on the porch!" Our back porch was so visible to us while sitting at the dining table. I immediately turned to look, and sure enough, there he was a five- or six-foot slender black snake, crawling up on our porch. Gayle then commented that he was young, assuming that because he was so slender. Long but not big around.

Now we knew that black snakes are not poisonous, not a danger to humans, likely prey on mice; but despite that knowledge, we had no pleasure in seeing a snake of any kind on our porch.

Just the word *snake* gives no warm or pleasurable feeling to most people. The sight of a snake nearby disturbs us even more. Snakes just have a bad reputation. Ever since Adam and Eve. Generally speaking, we have no friendly feelings for the slithering, crawling creature.

Not wanting to kill him, but anxious to have him go away, I grabbed my strong windy blower, aiming it at him. He crawled away, out of sight, likely under the house.

Thought. Reputation is important! Sometimes a person may not be actually doing anything wrong, but their *reputation bothers us. We are very uncomfortable in their presence.*

> A good reputation and respect are worth much more than silver and gold. (Proverbs 22:1 CEV)

Know There Is Restored
Power in Pause

❧❦❧

It was still springtime, the morning part of the day. The air was a bit crisp. The breeze was gentle. It was light, but the sun was not all heated up bearing down on me.

I was seated in my backyard, quietly observing. There in front of me were my small white water rapids flowing down what looked like a mountain stream falling over many gray rocks. The water fell softly into our green lily pad-covered goldfish pond. Standing proudly in the midst of the green lily pads was one single yellow lily bloom. Beautiful, as if dressing up the whole pond. The pond water was still and calm with a glassy surface.

Around this oasis-like area, all in full view, in my backyard, are pink and red flowers and lots of gorgeous green ferns.

All of this picturesque scenery is there for me, and the gray squirrels, and the red birds. At no cost. Someone visiting us recently said, "If I had this backyard, I would never get anything done. I would just sit here." She meant to enjoy the scenery, viewing and listening to the white water rapids falling across the rocks.

Thought. Sometimes what our body, mind, and spirit need is to do nothing but sit, observe, and listen. Thinking, quietly, alone, on encouraging words from the Bible.

> The Lord is my Shepherd; I shall not want.
> He maketh me to lie down in green pastures: He
> leadeth me beside the still waters. He restoreth
> my soul. (Psalm 23:1–3 KJV)

Be Kind to Animals

Our son, Wayne, is trying to tame two wild horses. They are small but larger than a pony. He sort of inherited these horses that live on their own, unattended, in a pasture, bordering some land he recently purchased. The owner of the neighboring land told Wayne that he didn't even know if the horses were still alive. Evidently, their grazing land was so large with natural water available that he, their owner, had just left them to themselves. No care.

But now that Wayne has learned about those horses. Seen them. Realized they have not been properly cared for. He's taken a personal interest. He's even taking responsibility for having a veterinarian and a farrier check them out. Do whatever they need for proper health care. And he's giving them treats to make friends. He wants to relate personally to the horses. Sounds to me that the previously wild horses are on their way to becoming tamed and friendly, with better care from their new neighbor. And Wayne seems to be having fun building a relationship with the little guys.

I'm not surprised. Wayne has always loved animals. Dogs. Cats. Goats. Rabbits, which he currently owns, and a dog that loves him.

Thought. How people treat their animals reveals a lot about their character.

Good people are kind to their animals. (Proverbs 12:10 CEV)

For every beast of the forest is mine, and the cattle upon a thousand hills. (Psalm 50:10 KJV)

Have a Sound and Balanced Mind

◈◈◈

When I was a student at the University of Georgia, working on my master's in social work, I studied the work of Sigmund Freud, the father of modern-day psychology.

At New Orleans Baptist Theological Seminary and Eastern Baptist Theological Seminary, in Philadelphia, I studied the Bible.

Both Freud and the Bible complement each other at times and help in understanding the human mind and personality.

Freud said our personality has three parts. The id. The ego. And the superego. As I understand his writings, the id is the part that includes our source of energy, creativity, playfulness, and sexuality. The superego is our conscience, our guard, boundaries, knowing right from wrong. *Our ego is the source of "I am" and "I can."* It should be in charge most of the time. If all three are balanced, that's a healthy sound mind and a right mind.

The apostle Paul revealed a sound and balanced mind when he said of himself, "*I (my ego) can do all things through Christ which strengtheneth me*" (Philippians 4:13 KJV).

A faith relationship with God through Jesus Christ helps us to have a sound and balanced mind.

> For God hath not given us the spirit of fear;
> but of power and of love, and of a sound mind.
> (2 Timothy 1:7 KJV)

Pause Can Have Purpose

I t's amazing how God may speak to us from time to time through a Christian friend.

Recently, we had a friend visit us from California. In the course of her time with us, Gayle and I, in our home, she said, "You're on a sabbatical now, and you shouldn't get off it too soon." She was referring to my resting and not teaching the Bible in Sunday school for the past several months. That began with the COVID pandemic.

I often wondered why is resting, not moving, not doing, not involvement so difficult for some of us? It's like I have no purpose without being busy. No meaningfulness. As if "being still" is the same as total worthlessness. Even to question the need for a Sabbath.

Yet, Almighty God, the Creator of the Universe, rested on the seventh day.

"Be still, rest, and relax" are meaningful and have a purpose. We need to reread some scriptures and think about them.

Thought. Stop, look, and listen are wise words. Pause times can be creative times.

> Remember the Sabbath day to keep it holy. (Exodus 20:8 KJV)

> Come unto Me, all ye that labour and are heavy laden and I will give you rest... And ye shall find rest unto your souls. (Matthew 11:28–29 KJV)

Love Yourself

He is an attorney and a friend of mine. We stay in touch by phone. He has been a help and encourager to me. And he has indicated that a few times, I have been of help to him, an encourager to each other for several years.

Just recently in a casual conversation, I reminded him that *Jesus said, "Love your neighbor as yourself," not instead of yourself.* He responded that he had never thought of it that way and thanked me for the encouraging words.

Several thoughts you may or we all may be reminded that it's okay to love yourself. In fact, the opposite of that is not good. Not to have a healthy sense of loving yourself can be destructive to your mind and body. Not haughty arrogance but a wise common sense, a healthy sense of self. Love yourself. Your mind. Your body. God has given you only oneself. Take care of it. As a gift from God.

Living wisely. Common sense thoughts, words, activity. These are ways of loving yourself as God wants you to. Reading the Bible daily, especially Proverbs, teaches us how to do this.

> You surely know that your body is a temple where the Holy Spirit lives. The Spirit is in you and is a gift from God. You are no longer your own. God paid a great price for you. So use your body to honor God. (1 Corinthians 6:19 CEV)

> We love because God loved us first. (1 John 4:19 CEV)

Think how much the Father loves us. He loves us so much that He lets us be called His children as we truly are. (1 John 3:1 CEV)

Choose Your Friends Carefully

꧁꧂

Twinky is a beautifully colored cat with stripes of orange, brown, black, and white. Truly a pretty and well-mannered little creature. Her primary owner is Amy, our granddaughter. You don't have to question whom the cat loves the most. She permits Amy to hold her like a baby, and she cuddles in Amy's arms.

And Twinky makes it clear that she is selective about whom she permits to pet her or even come near her. She likes to stay in Amy's bedroom and sleep on Amy's bed.

Twinky can be very singular-minded, well-defining whom she accompanies, whom she's friendly with, and where she hangs out and spends her leisure time.

Both Amy and Twinky are certain about their relationship. They know and the people around them know by observation the loyal, caring, devoted, and trusting relationship between the cat and her owner. No questions about it.

Point: We humans might learn a few lessons from Twinky like whom we spend time with, whom our close friends are, and whom we are loyal to.

> He that walketh with wise men shall be
> wise: but a companion of fools shall be destroyed.
> (Proverbs 13:20 KJV)

Reading the Bible daily, especially Psalm 1 and Proverbs, teaches us how to choose friends wisely!

Keep Good Friends

❧❧❧

Burnis Barrett will be ninety years old on March 4, 2021. He lives in Frederick, Maryland. One of his three daughters Jane called me a few days ago and reminded me of his birthday.

Burnis and Clotene, his wife who has already gone to be with the Lord, have two other daughters, Robin, the oldest, and Cheryl, the youngest.

While Burnis lives alone in an assisted living apartment, the daughters are still very involved in his care.

Jane, when she called, asked if I would recall and write some memories I have of yesteryears with Burnis. That was an easy assignment. I've known Burnis some fifty or sixty years.

The main thing I remember of my experiences with Burnis is his humor. He was always good for a great laugh. He is a Baptist minister. *He could have been a second Bob Hope!*

He could also tell a *scary story.* Making you believe all the time that he was telling a true story.

He could also tell you of a *very serious story, full of romance.* Like when he was in college and first saw Clotene and wanted to date her.

He could also almost bring tears to my eyes when he once told me of his childhood and early years in Mississippi. As I recall, his mother died, and his father felt compelled to give up all the children to live in an orphan's home.

Anyway, Burnis is a fun guy, a Christian, a minister, a father, and a husband by whom I have been honored to be *one of his many friends.*

> The lamp of a good person keeps on shining. (Proverbs 13:9 CEV)

Remember the Grace of God

❧

John Newton (1725–1807) was not a nice guy in the early part of his life. He was known to be a slave trader. Buying and selling human beings. His mother died when he was about eleven years old. Being only with his father was not good for parenting him.

Evidently, according to historical information of his life, it was a frightening storm at sea that put the fear of God in him. He cried out for God's mercy, forgiveness, and grace.

It was sometime after this spiritual experience at sea that he wrote the famous Christian hymn, "Amazing Grace."

"Amazing grace how sweet the sound that saved a wretch like me," he wrote.

A very dear person to me and to our entire family recently wrote to me, marveling about the "amazing grace of God" in her life. Exclaiming and praising God for His grace toward her. Because of where she had been and so forth, she "should be dead." Drugs. Alcohol.

The truth of the matter is, whether admitted or not, we all need and are so dependent on God's grace!

But the good news is that when anyone of us humbly approaches God, like this dear person I mentioned and like John Newton, regardless of the desperate and ugly past, *God forgives when we cry out to Him for help. Mercy. Grace. Forgiveness.*

> For by grace are ye saved through faith;
> and that not of yourselves; it is the gift of God.
> (Ephesians 2:8 KJV)

Finish Well

He said in the midst of our conversation, "I want to finish well." He is a man, in fact, a longtime minister, married for over fifty years, realizing his mortality.

What about that statement, "I want to finish well"? There are several components to the statement.

One is that it is much easier to start something than to finish it. It's easy to bring a child into this world. It's not as easy to raise a child. It may be easy to enlist or start a job. Not as easy to stay with it and complete it. The place and point where a young person signs up to enlist are totally different from the basic training and the battlefield.

Saying, "Yes, I want to be a Christian and follow Christ," is easier said than following Christ for a lifetime. Also, there is the fact that as we get older, our physical and mental capabilities lessen. As another friend of mine once said, "Getting old is not for sissies."

So as my friend said, "I want to finish well," it is definitely something we all face in every area of our lives.

Finishing well is a great challenge. I recall in high school cross-country racing, the last few minutes of the race was definitely the hardest. It took determination! Willpower! *Keeping my eyes and mind on the goal, the finish line, was the motivating factor that kept me in the race. So is true in life. Eternity.*

The apostle Paul said:

> I have fought well. I have finished the race, and I have been faithful. So a crown will be give to me for pleasing the Lord. (2 Timothy 4:7–8 CEV)

Realize the Value of Today

⚜

S he said to me on the phone, "They used the paddles on him [her dad] again today." That meant that he flatlined again. Code blue. He is in the hospital. The *again* meant that he has died twice, and the doctors have brought him back to life twice in the past few days of July 2021.

The person informing me was the daughter of a dear friend of mine. The doctors have already told them there's nothing else they can do for him. And that it seems *"he's not going to make it."* Interpreted meaning, his heart is very bad. He's going to die and stay dead soon. He doesn't have much time left to live on this earth. He's going to leave his wife, his children, and his grandchildren probably very soon.

No more sitting around the table eating with them. No more enjoying moments of sharing stories and laughing together.

Thought to consider: How important your *now* is. The *present tense*. Today. I, you, *none of us can relive yesterday*. We can't jump forward and live in tomorrow. *All we have is now!* This very moment! *How valuable is today!*

Tell someone you love them. Give a gift to a friend, a loved one, or a total stranger. Smile at someone as they pass by. Can't reach into tomorrow. Tomorrow is a day away. All we have is this moment! Life is fragile! *One day, each of us "won't make it!"*

> For what is your life? It is even a vapour, that appeareth for a little time, and then vanisheth away! (James 4:14 KJV)

> Behold, now is the accepted time; behold, now is the day of salvation. (2 Corinthians 6:26)

Realize Our Faith Is to
Be Continuous

~~~~~

The one verse that is likely most well-known in the New Testament is John 3:16. It is quoted frequently as the way to get to know God personally and for God to get to know you.

> For God so loved the world that He gave His only begotten Son, that whosoever believeth in Him should not perish, but have everlasting life. (John 3:16 KJV)

The Greek word in the original language translated *believeth* means "to entrust and commit to the change of power of."

Somewhat like a soldier committing and entrusting his life to be surrendered to another authority.

In the same chapter (chapter 3), verses 15, 16, and 18, the same word *believeth* is used four times. These four words in the original language (Greek) are all present indicative active participles. What that means is that *this believing, this entrusting, this committing is ongoing! Continuous! Durative! It's not just a one-time, one-moment, one-hour, or one-day experience! There is an adamant and clear meaning that it's to be continuous for your whole life! If it's not continuous, it's not real! Not authentic! Not valid!*

Thought. For more on this, I encourage you to read in your Bible Matthew chapter 13. This is an important chapter for all of us to read carefully.

Reading the Bible daily helps us to be continuously committed and trusting in our relationship with God, especially Proverbs.

You Can Love Even into Your Senior Years

The psalmist said, "This is the day the Lord hath made: We will rejoice and be glad in it."

The fact of the matter was, I slept late that morning. Lay in bed until 9:45 a.m., a few hours after I had awakened. I had nothing on my schedule for the day. Just had to get up, get dressed, and feed my squirrels and goldfish in our backyard pond. Nothing being on my mind that was urgent, I just decided to lay there, mind clear, quiet time. My only awareness was that my wife of sixty-four years was at my side. Both of us are very much into our senior years. But the intensity of the moment was that I was aware of her presence. Touching me. At my side. How blessed and thankful I was to feel the warmth of her touch. Both of us are healthy and still very much alert.

Years from now, as some of my children or grandchildren read this. I hope you, too, will still be in love with your spouse even into your senior years. Love can stay alive if you feed it, prayerfully and thoughtfully daily.

Thought. Even into your eighties, there may not be any ordinary days. Every day is a gift. And it is a very special gift with the one you love at your side.

> This is the day the Lord hath made. We will rejoice and be glad in it. (Psalm 118:24 KJV)

> Who can find a virtuous woman... The heart of her husband doth safely trust in her... she will do him good and not evil all the days of her life. (Proverbs 31:10–12 KJV)

Be happy with the wife you married when you were young. She is beautiful and graceful, just like a deer; you should be attracted to her and stay deeply in love. (Proverbs 5:18–19 CEV)

Fear Your Heavenly Father

The years between 1940 and 1953 were the years that I remember vividly as my school years. From the first grade of elementary school to my graduation from high school, the twelfth grade. Those were the years of my growing up in a feared relationship with my father. He disciplined my brother Larry and me with a few whippings. Not paddling. Whippings. With his belt. He also disciplined with a stern look that I feared all my school years.

He made clear to me where the boundary lines were, defining good and evil. Right and wrong. And the consequences of doing wrong.

So actually, I received very few disciplines with his belt because of my inward fear of the consequences. I admit that *a sense of fear or respect kept me within safe and healthy boundaries most of the time.* It was for my own good.

Throughout life, in my adulthood, I have reaped the rewards of a healthy fear not of my earthly father, but of my Heavenly Father, And I have felt His discipline at times. That kind of fear is a wise and good thing!

> The fear of the Lord is the beginning of knowledge, but fools despise wisdom and instruction. (Proverbs 1:7 KJV)

> And fear not them which kill the body, but are not able to kill the soul; but rather fear Him which is able to destroy both soul and body in hell. (Matthew 10:28 KJV)

Women, Read the Bible Daily

A few days ago, right in the middle of this July summer in Georgia, I was corresponding with my sister Sylvia and her husband, Herman. In fact, I shared that I thought Sylvia had the best husband in the whole family.

Through Sylvia's many health problems, Herman has been a devoted husband.

I give him a five-star rating or an *A+* from an academic perspective. I've always thought that and heard that our own parents rated Herman the same way. Any time I ever heard any one of the family speak of Herman, it was always positive and with a smile.

I suppose since my sister, Sylvia, was a school teacher, she had that ability and wisdom to recognize and choose an *A+* husband. I'm not sure *A+* husbands are made. They may be just born that way. Some of us are *C*'s on our good days and maybe a *C+* at our best. Just the way it is.

I recall being in the fourth grade, back in the old days. Getting a paddling at school with five other peers. Paddled for failing a test, but the teacher said, "I guess you all noticed that Warren got less of a paddling than you, others, because I know he really tried."

I interpreted that to mean that some of us just don't have it in us to be as good as others.

Reading the Bible daily will definitely give wisdom to women in choosing their husbands.

A husband should love his wife as much as
Christ loved the Church and gave His life for it.
(Ephesians 5:25 CEV)

Take Care of Your Body

Not one of those phone calls anyone wants to receive. She said to me, "I'm in the hospital. Will you come see me?" Her story went something like this. "My landlord found me unconscious in my apartment last Thursday. He called 911. They brought me here. I had overdosed." This was not the first time that she had done such. In fact, this was about the fourth or fifth time in the past ten years.

Anyway, the twenty-nine-year-old young lady was the one telling about herself. She went on to tell me that her physical diagnosis was even worse. "Doctors tell me that I have the heart of an eighty-year-old man."

In the past ten years, she has abused all sorts of drugs and alcohol. She has virtually worn out her body. Self-destruction of her own choosing. Despite all the warning signs that began ten years ago.

Why would anyone do that to themselves? The *why* is the cry and the plea to her from her family. Her parents, grandparents, sisters, and loved ones. The cry is not a soft whisper. It is the screaming cries from many broken hearts.

Don't do it! Don't even think of doing it to yourself! Love yourself! Know that God loves you. You have only one body for this lifetime.

> You surely know that your body is a temple where the Holy Spirit lives. The Spirit is in you and is a gift from God. You are no longer your own. God paid a great price for you. So use your body to honor God. (1 Corinthians 6:19–20 CEV)

Pray for a Place where You Fit Well

∽◟◠◡◟◠◡∾

It's a very special word, *place*. It's a word that has fascinated me through the years. Maybe because Jesus said, as we read in John 14:3 (JKV), "*And if I go and prepare a place for you, I will come again.*"

I've lived in different places throughout my life. I grew up in South Georgia; moved to Carlisle, Pennsylvania, for five years; then lived in Crisfield, Maryland, for five years. I then moved to Pasadena, Maryland, near Annapolis and Baltimore for ten years. I also lived in New Orleans for three years.

At every place, there were different experiences. Two daughters were born in New Orleans, Linda in 1959 and Dianne in 1961. Two sons were born in Carlisle, Pennsylvania: Alan in 1965 and Wayne in 1966.

However, *place* may refer not only to *where* I am geographically but also to *how* I am emotionally or spiritually. Am I in a place of strength or weakness or even brokenness? Place of joy or sadness. Good or not so good.

Reading the Bible daily definitely helps us to be in a good place mentally, emotionally, and spiritually regardless of what place we may be in geographically, especially Psalm 1 and Proverbs.

> Not that I speak in respect of want, for I
> have learned in whatsoever state *I* am therewith
> to be content. (Philippians 4:11 KJV)

Give at Least 10 Percent, the Tithe

∼⊙⊙∽

The year was 1957. I was a student at Mercer University in Macon, about to graduate in June. I had been a student there for two years, majoring in Christianity and minoring in English. The courses I enjoyed most were Greek, taught by Dr. Ed Johnston. He was a tough but great professor. I recall classes with Jerry, who later was at our wedding in Omega.

Gayle was a junior at Mercer during my senior year. So she had another year. We got married the same week I graduated.

The point I want to bring to your attention is that I had a major problem with money. I needed a sum of over $300 in order to graduate. Without the money, I couldn't graduate. I knew I couldn't get the money from Dad. He didn't have it, so I borrowed it from a layman in Byron Harbin's church. Byron was a longtime friend of mine. He worked out the deal for me.

But all in all, it was an example of how God has all my life provided for me and my family financially. Always. I believe His provision has been based on my faith in the idea and teaching of tithing. Gayle and I have always given at least 10 percent.

> Bring ye all the tithes into the storehouse, that there may be meat in mine house, and prove Me now herewith saith the Lord of Hosts, if I will not open you the windows of heaven and pour you out a blessing, that there shall not be room enough to receive it. (Malachi 3:10 KJV)

> Remember the words of the Lord Jesus, how he said It is more blessed to give than to receive. (Acts 20:35 KJV)

Definitely Keep Your Humor Alive

This happened when my mom and dad were both still living in Eastman. Gayle and I were on our way to visit them, driving from Augusta. It must have been early or late in the fall because the cotton was white in fields ready and waiting to be picked.

As we were passing one very white field, both of us observing, I said to Gayle, "Did I ever tell you that I was born in a cotton field?"

Gayle quickly responded, "Warren, you never told me that!"

Then I said, "Yes, Mother went into labor with me when she was out picking cotton. I was born on a pile of cotton."

Again, Gayle responded, fully believing my story and acting very surprised, "Warren, you never told me that before!"

Of course, it wasn't true! I just spontaneously made the story up. Motivated, I guess by all the cotton fields. It sounded like a good story to me at the moment. Anyway, for several minutes, I contained my laughter before it just couldn't be held in! Bursting into laughter, not her, I told her that I had just made the story up.

Somewhat, not entirely, she seemingly interpreted all of it as a lie. Not a story. But we did, both of us, laugh about it then and many times years later. And that laughter has been a continuing and very viable part of our marriage relationship for all our years together. I'm glad. And yes, she does get revenge for my made-up stories.

> A merry heart maketh a cheerful countenance: but by sorrow of the heart the spirit is broken. (Proverbs 15:13 KJV)

Consider the Tears of Others

⁓⊙⊙⁓

It was a very cold, cloudy wintry day in that Pennsylvania country-side cemetery. It felt like a very lonely place. Below freezing, snow covered the ground. White everywhere. Weary-eyed folks standing around the gravesite. Tears. Somber faces. Hovering together in the quiet. Sad parents about to bury their six-year-old son. I was the minister officiating. This was in 1965 while I was the pastor of Carlisle Baptist Church.

I had known the poor family months before. They lived in an old red brick farmhouse in the country. I had visited their home several times since their six-year-old son had been sent home from the hospital. Brain tumor. Doctors said there was nothing else they could do. The prognosis was that the tumor would gradually blind him. It did. Then he would die after suffering from blindness for months. And so it was! All of it was gradual. A very slow death!

There is no way we humans can make any sense of such a situation! *While we may not be able to gain answers to the whys, we may find some comfort and hope by reading the Bible.*

> And God will wipe away every tear from their eyes! "There shall be no more death, nor sorrow, nor crying. (Revelation 21:4 KJV)

> Yea though I walk through the valley of the shadow of death, I will fear no evil for Thou art with me; Thy rod and Thy staff they comfort me. (Psalm 23:4 KJV)

Remember that You
Too Are Mortal

～◌◌◌～

There we were. All five of us, his children. Three sons. Two daughters. We stood semicircle at the foot of Dad's bed. He was almost eighty-six. 1997. Dying. Breathing his last breaths. We knew it. Not a word was being said. Silent. Total silence. Dad was still breathing. Very shallow breaths. But his eyes were closed. He was already unconscious.

We, all five, had gathered there quietly, about thirty minutes before he died. Peacefully in his own bed, at home. In Dodge County, Georgia. The county where he was born in 1911.

He had lived through two great wars, World War I and World War II. The Great Depression in the 1930s. He was a country bivocational Baptist preacher. A rural mail carrier, married to our mother for sixty years.

Moments like that, we never forget! Written in our memories like words etched in stone.

Reading the Bible daily helps us to accept and to comfort ourselves in the loss of a loved one and to prepare us as we realize our own mortality!

> God loved the people of this world so much
> that He gave His only Son, so that everyone who
> has faith in Him will have eternal life and never
> really die. (John 3:16 CEV)

> Blessed are the dead which die in the Lord.
> (Revelation 14:13 KJV)

Realize You May Not Be
as Bad as You Feel

ᕀᏬᏬᏬ

I t was no special day, just ordinary, but the fact that I woke up at 6:30 a.m. did make it different. I usually sleep later in my senior year.

But it had become a special moment when my wife was standing by our bed, looking down at me lying there, laughing at me. Yes, laughing as she held a thermometer, having just taken my temperature.

I had awakened earlier, thinking I was sick, not feeling well, so she had taken my temperature.

Now laughing because the thermometer informed her that I had NO temperature. She sort of thinks that I actually enjoy being sick and having her wait on me.

Her laughter was in essence saying to me, *"You're not sick. I know you're disappointed!"*

Then I said, "If I'm not sick, I guess I'll just need to get up! No need to keep lying here."

Thought. Often things are not as bad as we feel they are. Our feelings can't always be trusted. It's good to have someone with you to see the lighter side of life and even laugh. My wife is good at that. When it comes to sickness, life in general, she is able to stay positive.

> A merry heart doeth good like a medicine.
> (Proverbs 17:22 CEV)

> Kind words are good medicine. (Proverbs 15:4 CEV)

> A helpful wife is a jewel for her husband. (Proverbs 12:4 CEV)

Look Forward to Your Eternal Home

❧◎❧

December 17, 2020, was the day Uncle Delton died. He was eighty-seven years old. I knew him well as a kid. We worked in the fields together for three consecutive summers—1943, 1944, and 1945. The Junes. The Julys. The Augusts. We hoed peanuts. Dropped fertilizer by hand to corn in the *hot South Georgia sun.*

There were often five of us who worked together all day. There was Delton, his older sisters, Jean and Clara, and my younger brother, Larry.

All four of them are now gone. I'm the only one left. Delton, who never moved away from the farm, was born in 1933. He was the youngest of twelve children given birth by my grandmother. My dad was the oldest born in 1911. Thus, it is the end of an era. All twelve are gone. Collectively, they lived from 1911 to 2020. One hundred and nine years.

The last time I spoke to Delton was immediately after the 2020 Presidential Election. We both agreed with our disappointment over the election results. *However,* the next time we meet and talk, there will be *no hot sun and no disappointments! Heaven!*

> Jesus said, "Let not your heart be troubled: ye believe in God, believe also in Me." (John 14:1 KJV)

> And the city did not need the sun or the moon. The glory of God was shining on it, and the Lamb was its light. Revelation 21:23 CEV

Believe the Bible Is God's Word

c&o&v&

"**D**idn't men write the Bible!" It was said more like the tone of a statement! Rather than a question. This was a recent college graduate, who seems very aware of her accomplishment.

I've often said that those are the smartest years of one's life. College graduate. Single. In their twenties. Very little experience with life.

The problems. The headaches. Working at a job full time. Day in, day out. Being married. Raising children. Family. *Not!*

Anyway, the statement, "Didn't men write the Bible," had the sound of doubting its validity and authenticity.

I suppose many, maybe most, must settle that question in their own minds. *Do I believe the Bible is in fact the Word of God* to man through the minds of men?

We call that faith! Do I choose to believe the Bible or not believe it? It is a decision we each must make. I understand that even Billy Graham had to wrestle with and prayerfully struggle in order to settle that question in his own mind.

> All Scripture is given by inspiration of God. (2 Timothy 3:16 KJV)

> Then He (Jesus) said unto them, "O fools, and *slow of heart to believe* all that the prophets have spoken." (Luke 24:25 KJV)

> He (Jesus) came unto His own, and His own received Him not. But as many as received, Him to them gave He power to become the sons of God, even to them that believe on His name. (John 1:11–12 KJV)

Pray Personally for Yourself

*T*he *first time* I really can remember actually praying was as an eight-year-old kid at my grandfather's farm, near Rhine, Georgia. I was homesick, praying every night for my mother and dad to come to get me. They always did at the end of summer, but not before.

The second time I recall actually praying, I mean seriously, was as a teenager while delivering newspapers in Abbeville, Georgia, early every morning before daylight. I would be walking, throwing newspapers on porches, praying out loud. I don't recall what I was praying about, just praying, talking out loud to God.

Now years later, as an adult, I pray mainly for our children and grandchildren and their families, daily, by name. I believe that my most heartfelt prayers are now. But those early prayers, as a child, then as a teenager, were sincere and earnest.

But one thing different now, as an adult in my older years, is that I also pray more personally for myself—to think, speak, and do right. For God's help. Wisdom. His guidance. Daily. David did.

He prayed:

> You are my God. Show me what You want me to do, and let your gentle Spirit lead me in the right path. (Psalm 143:10 CEV)

He prayed:

> Let the words of my mouth, and the meditation of my heart, be acceptable in thy sight, O Lord, my strength, and my Redeemer. (Psalm 19:14 KJV)

Be Aware that You Do Have Purpose

❧◉◎◐

It was a sunny day, toward the end of summer, a few days before Labor Day. While sunny, it was not as hot as it had been, so that felt good. I was standing in our front yard watering some flowers.

The big difference was that my daughter-in-law and her daughter, my grandchild, were there visiting with us and, at that moment, conversing with me about life. My old age, in my eighties, and my purpose.

I had started the conversation by saying something like, "I don't really know my purpose at this time in my life." Suddenly, she became teary-eyed, saying, "You do have a purpose. You are a help to your son, Wayne, my husband, when you talk together by phone."

Honestly, I had not even thought that our conversations had been that meaningful or helpful. To me, yes. But not to him. He is very smart, level-headed, and has always been very wise even from his youth.

But it was encouraging for me to hear her say, "Yes, you have a purpose for your family."

Thought. Seemingly, *just being present and available, with a listening ear, is purposeful and meaningful to others.*

Jesus said

> Then the ones who pleased the Lord will ask, "When did we give you something to eat or drink? When did we welcome you as a stranger or give you clothes to wear or visit you while you were sick or in jail." (Matthew 25:35–36)

The King will answer, "Whenever you did it for any of my people, no matter how unimportant they seemed, you did it for me." (Matthew 25:37–40 CEV)

Realize the Healing Power in Caring Eyes and a Gentle Touch

S he looked at me with her big brown caring eyes. She touched my hand and arm with a gentle touch.

She was a nurse, likely in her twenties. I was her eighty-five-year-old patient. I was in the Moultrie, Georgia, hospital emergency room. My heart was out of rhythm, my pulse was at 150 and fluttering. I was helplessly in the care of other people. I was totally out of my element. Those people did not know me. I just introduced my name a few minutes ago. The doctor was Dr. Klar. The young nurse was Heidi.

Within a few hours with their wisdom and professional knowledge, they caused my heart to be *converted* back in rhythm and have a normal pulse.

I responded verbally to them, "You are miracle workers!" The warm, caring eyes. The gentle touch. There is healing in warm, caring eyes and a gentle touch. I was paying for their professional services. The other was *their free gift to me.*

It's a wonderful part of life when we receive and when we give warm caring eyes and a gentle touch to one another. It's really something money cannot buy. *It's either free, or it doesn't exist.*

It's also good to know that God looks at me and you with caring eyes. His gentle touch is always available. May we return our look up to Him.

> I will lift up mine eyes unto the hills from whence cometh my help. My help cometh from the Lord which made heaven and earth. (Psalm 121:1–2 KJV)

Jesus touched their eyes and said, "Because of your faith, you will be healed." (Matthew 9:29 CEV)

Don't Give Up—You Can Get Up

❧

He said it so strongly that it has rung in my ears and mind for years afterward. *"Is there anything good in this marriage?"* He was a college school therapist, a counselor, for college students. It was me and my wife who he was addressing the question. We were just sitting there wide-eyed and open ears because it made me stop and give the question some serious thought.

Actually, I was a full-time student in graduate school for the third time. This time at the University of Georgia. Gayle and I had been through some rough changes. Geographical change. Emotionally, I was not in good shape. So it had threatened our relationship. We had gone to see this counselor.

That one question shocked me into thinking. Yes, there is a lot of good in this marriage. *I will not let it fail or crumble! Too much at stake!*

Thought. So what can one do in times like these? There is no question whether such storms in your life will come. They may happen to the very best of people. Good or bad. Tough times. Uphill climbs. Deep valleys. They are part of life. *I decided not to give up. You too can decide to get up, not give up.* The battle is in your mind.

One verse of Scripture that I have memorized and thought on over the years has helped me many times to find the inward strength to *"get up." It is possible!*

> The Lord is my light and my salvation;
> whom shall I fear? The Lord is the strength of my
> life; of whom shall *I* be afraid? (Psalm 27:1 KJV)

Realize Life May Become Complicated

ec∞∞v

June of 1957, how simple it was! How different it was for me *then, compared to my now of June 2020.* Of course, I am older, much older. Then, in June of 1957, Gayle and I were just married. We lived in a small rented apartment in Macon, Georgia. She was a stay-at-home bride. I had a job at Inland Container, a box-building factory in Macon. We owned nothing, except for the one forty-nine, black two-door Chevrolet I had when we got married.

I worked at Inland Container for three months, the entire summer, June, July, and August, before beginning my teaching job in September. The job at Inland was hot, hard, manual labor!

But life was very simple! Just the two of us, my young beautiful twenty-year-old wife and me at twenty-two years. No kids. No grandkids. No great-grandkids. All four of our parents, moms and dads, were still alive and healthy. We were young, so our memory banks were also small and simple.

Today, June 2020. The changes would fill volumes. Maybe that's why greater wisdom is supposedly and hopefully given to us as we grow old and older. Our hands and our minds become so much fuller. Crowded. So much more complicated. We need more wisdom. Much more!

> Remember now thy Creator in the days of thy youth, while the evil days come not, nor thy years draw nigh. (Ecclesiastes 12:1)

> He that getteth wisdom loveth his own soul. (Proverbs 19:8 KJV)

Think from Youth to Old Age to the Future

⋘৩৩⋙

Read Psalm 71 about being young and being old. The contrast between the two. Youth versus old age. When you're young, at least for myself, I don't recall even thinking about getting old. I guess I thought that time and age just stood still.

But seemingly, almost suddenly, I'm old. I think, *How did I get here so fast!* Looking back over the years, I realize much has happened. Been many places, many states, many cities. Met many people. So many of them are already gone. It seems unbelievable. My life from birth to old age went by like a flash of lightning. Whether I believe it or not, it's true. It's my life, not my grandparent's. Not even my parents. Me. Myself.

I'm thankful to still be here. With my wife. Four grown children. Eight grandchildren. Three great-grandchildren. Very few regrets. Looking toward my future. *Alive with Him!*

Think. Your life will also go by quickly. Be careful with your NOW! Read your Bible every day. Psalm 1 and Proverbs.

> I depend on You, I have trusted You since I was young. I have relied on You from the day I was born. You brought me safely through birth, and **I** always praise You. (Psalm 71:5–6 CEV)

> Don't throw me aside when I am old, don't desert me when my strength is gone. (Psalm 71:9 CEV)

Reaching forth unto those things which are before, I press toward the mark for the prize of the high calling of God in Christ Jesus. (Philippians 3:13–14 KJV)

Realize Every Tenant's
Lease Comes to an End

cↄⓄⓇↄↄ

His voice was very soft when he said to me, affirming, "*I want you and my son [who is a Methodist minister] to do the main part of my funeral.*" Byron is eighty-eight years old, born in South Georgia in 1933, two years before me.

I first met Byron in junior college in Norman Park, Georgia. We both were single, youngsters, planning to go into the Christian ministry. We continued our education together at Mercer University in Macon, Georgia, and then at New Orleans Baptist Theological Seminary.

Later, for several years, I went into what was called Pioneer Missions for Southern Baptists in Carlisle, Pennsylvania. Byron served thirty years in Brazil as a Southern Baptist Foreign Missionary.

Now we're both retired. Me in Georgia. Byron, with his wife, Dora, is in an assisted living facility in Mississippi. But we both have stayed in touch for over sixty years.

Byron knows that the bottom line in life on this earth is, *our lease is almost up.* We have been tenants here for eighty-plus years each. Nothing of what we have gained materially that may look like success can be taken with us. We came in empty-handed. We leave empty-handed. That's the bottom line!

The only ultimate success at this point is having a personal faith in Jesus Christ our Lord.

You can never pay God enough to stay alive
forever and safe from death. (Psalm 49:8–9 CEV)

Accept It—Being Old
Is Different

かのひん

Question: Is *just being* important? Significant in the eyes of God? Being has to do with one's heart, our motives, our character, our thoughts. It is who we are, not what we do. It's more than a title or a position.

In my old age, without a job, I have no daily schedule that a job demands. No definite expectations. Only those I myself or my wife suggest to me. So at the end of the day, I have not necessarily completed any full day's assignment. There's no field I can look back at and say to myself, "I plowed." No row of peanuts I've hoed. No cotton I've picked. No visible evidence of accomplishment.

The day has been spent *being*. Maybe I've prayed a while. Read my Bible for a while. Studied. But there is no visible evidence of how I spent the past twenty-four hours.

So I call it *just being*. Being alive. Relating. To my wife and a few others, sometimes in person, sometimes just on the phone. I didn't earn any money. No increase in status, position, or power. At the end of the day, I have nothing in hand more than I had at dawn.

Do my thoughts? My prayers? My concerns for my family and friends count? Only God, I suppose, can answer that question.

> Remember now thy Creator in the days of
> thy youth, while the evil days come not nor the
> years draw nigh, when thou shalt say, "I have no
> pleasure in them." (Ecclesiastes 12:1 KJV)

Reading the Bible daily, especially Proverbs, helps us find meaning-fulness at any age.

Remember that Life Is Short

⌒⌒⌒⌒

Just a few months ago, my wife, Gayle, and I were standing together in the Omega Cemetery in Georgia, observing our tombstones—hers and mine side by side. The white marble headstone reads "Warren and Gayle, married 1957." Individually, mine has "Read Bible Daily, Psalm 1" beneath my name, "Warren Wells Burnham, Born June 6, 1935." Hers has "God Loves You, John 3:16" beneath her name, "Gayle Hornbuckle Burnham, Born December 31, 1936."

I'm not sure when I stopped saying, "*If* I die," and changed it to, "*When* I die." Perhaps it was after my twenty-four-year-old granddaughter, Cara said to me, "*Poppy, you're not old, you are very old!*"

Another granddaughter, Erica, told me one day, "*Poppy, I'll soon be seven, then I'll be eight, then I'll be nine, then I'll be ten, and you'll be dead.*" Well, that time passed. She's over ten. I'm still here.

Death is certain. Nearer every day. Reading Psalm 23 and Psalm 1 doesn't take the sting out of death, but it helps us be ready.

> We can expect seventy years or maybe eighty, if we are healthy, but disappear. Even our best years bring trouble and sorrow. Suddenly our time is up and we disappear. (Psalm 90:10 CEV)

> Teach us to use wisely all the time we have. (Psalm 90:12 CEV)

Be Ready

୬ଡ଼ଡ଼ଡ଼

We were on the way to University Hospital. My daughter Dianne and me. She was driving. I was the passenger. We were in a hurry to get me to the emergency room. My pulse was 140 times a minute. Twice what it should be. My heart, they later informed me, was "out of rhythm." That's not good, to say it mildly. The doctors told me that such could "cause a blood clot or a heart attack." They didn't tell me, but I know that it may only take one heart attack to radically change my address from here to hereafter.

Nevertheless, as Dianne was driving me very hurriedly to the hospital, we both were realizing the seriousness of the moment. It was then, admittedly through tears, that I spoke some words. Caringly. "If." She also spoke some caring words.

Then I said, "If… I'm ready as much as I can be." At eighty-five years of age, the statement is a real possibility. I could be changing my residence in a very short time. Maybe within moments.

It all reminded me of a hymn we used to sing in church when I was much younger. *"Are You Ready?" Are you ready for Judgment Day? Are you ready? Are you ready?*

Something to think about! There is *no "if." It's "when!"* For me and you!

> Prepare to meet thy God. (Amos 4:12 KJV)

> God loved the people of the world so much that He gave His only Son, so that everyone who has faith in Him will have eternal life and never really die. (John 3:16 CEV)

You Can't Always Trust
Your Feelings
Learn to Listen to Wise People

⨳⟋⟍⊙⟍⟍⨳

The doctor was standing at the foot of my bed. I was lying there looking up at him eye to eye. I was in the hospital emergency room again. Just arrived several minutes before he asked me, "How do you feel?" My response I think surprised him when I said, "I feel okay. I feel fine."

He responded, paternally, as he patted me on the foot, smiling, "Keep feeling fine."

But the truth of the matter was I was not fine. I was not okay. My heart was out of rhythm. My pulse was 140. Twice what it should have been. How could I say that I felt okay, even fine, when physically that was not the true situation.

How was it possible for my physical condition to be as it was, but my feelings and thinking about the situation didn't match. My feelings were lying to me. My feelings were not trustworthy.

That's why I needed to be where I was, in the hospital for professional people, wise people, to find out the truth and help me.

Often in life, such may be the situation. We can't totally trust our own feelings. We may need help to find the truth and deal with it. *We need to listen to someone wiser and more knowledgeable than ourselves. Only a fool refuses to listen to the truth to his own demise and destruction.*

> If you have good sense, you will listen
> and obey; if all you do is talk foolishly, you will
> destroy yourself. (Proverbs 10:8 CEV)

Fools think they know what is best, but a sensible person listens to advice. (Proverbs 12:15 CEV)

With all your heart, you must trust the Lord, and not your own judgement. (Proverbs 3:5 CEV)

Remember My Eighty-Fifth Birthday Word to You (June 6, 1935–June 6, 2020)

⁓⊙⊙⁓

Yes, I am eighty-five years old. It's hard for me to believe so many years have happened so fast, like a flash. From my birth, my youth, my middle age, to my old age, to very-old age. Life is indeed very short. You, too, will be where I am much sooner than you expect.

Times have changed since my birth in 1935. My mother was only twenty-one. My dad was twenty-three. Franklin D. Roosevelt was President. The United States was still in the middle of the Great Depression. People including my parents were poor. Sharecroppers, I think, but definitely poor. I was born in a house, not a hospital, in Rhine, Georgia. I was my parent's first child of five. Mom said that I was so ugly as a baby that she was ashamed to carry me out! I almost died with diphtheria at eighteen months old.

Anyway, I urge you to listen to me briefly. I know a few things by experience. For sure, How do you make it in this life? A few words I want to share with you, my kids. My grandkids. My great-grandkids. My reader friends. *While I'm still with you!*

Although I have earned several degrees: a bachelor's, two master's, and a doctorate (Mercer University, New Orleans Baptist Theological Seminary, University of Georgia, and Eastern Baptist Theological Seminary in Philadelphia) respectively. More importantly, I have read ragged several Bibles. *Wisdom and character come only from God and His Word. The Bible!*

First, have a faith relationship with Jesus Christ, with God. Believe. Repent. Believe. Read John 3:16. Read Romans 10:9–10.

Secondly, read the Bible every day. Read Psalm 1 and a chapter in Proverbs daily. According to the date of the month, read that chapter in Proverbs.

Thirdly, pray daily for yourself and for your family. Pray for wisdom!

Fourthly and finally is regarding money. Pay the tithe—10 percent of your gross income—to your church that you attend weekly.

Life will not be easy! But if you choose to do these extremely important things, you will make it in life—here on earth and in eternity. IT'S YOUR CHOICE!

PS. You don't need alcohol, drugs, or tobacco. Not good for your health.

> To accept correction is wise, to reject it is stupid. The Lord likes everyone who lives right, but He punishes everyone who makes evil plans. Sin cannot offer security! *But if you live right, you will be as secure as a tree with deep roots.* (Proverbs 12:1–3 CEV)

Wisdom! My Goal for You!

❧◉◎◎◎❧

My basic and primary goal for you is to encourage you to read *Psalm 1* and a chapter in *Proverbs* from the Bible *every day*. Each day of the month, read that chapter.

Why? Because Psalm 1 gives very clear directions concerning right and wrong, good and bad. It encourages you to *follow God's path for your own good*. You gain! *You, yourself, gain by being good and godly rather than bad and ungodly!*

Reading Proverbs feeds your mind with wise thoughts. Wisdom! We know that it is a psychological and spiritual fact that a person's thoughts affect his or her behavior. We tend to act, to behave, to be, the way we think. *Wise thinking produces wise behavior.* It's just good common sense!

Wise people have better character.

Wise people are more successful.

Wise people are more productive.

> *Proverbs will teach you wisdom and self-control and how to understand sayings with deep meanings.* You will learn what is right and honest and fair. From these, an ordinary person can learn to be smart. (Proverbs 1:2–4 CEV)

> If you are already wise, you will become even wiser. (Proverbs 1:5)

> Respect and obey the Lord! This is the beginning of knowledge. Only a fool rejects wisdom and good advice. (Proverbs 1:7 CEV)

If you do not have a copy of the New Testament with Psalm and Proverbs in the Contemporary English Version, I encourage you to get one!

Starting Over Is Possible

❦

Epilogue

After over thirty years as a Baptist pastor, I changed careers at the age of fifty-three. After finishing graduate school at the University of Georgia, earning a master's in social work, and completing the clinical part at the Medical College of Georgia in Augusta, all my savings depleted, I borrowed $20,000 to begin my private practice as a psychotherapist.

After twenty-eight years as a psychotherapist, I retired on December 31, 2018, at the age of eighty-three.

God blessed me with great collaborative relationships with medical doctors, ministers, and many others in the Augusta community.

I was able to retire total debt-free. Living in a beautiful home in one of the nicest West Augusta communities. Living comfortably. Both my wife and I drive Lexus vehicles.

This has not meant in any way to claim how to get rich. But it is to declare that all the principles of how to be wise and successful are in the Bible, especially Psalm 1 and the book of Proverbs.

The reason they are there is that God gave them there through men. *"That it may be well with thee"* (Ephesians 6:3 KJV).

Therefore, I urge you to read the Bible daily, especially Psalm 1 and Proverbs! Think about it!

> And thou shalt do that which is right and
> good in the sight of the Lord: that it may be well
> with thee. (Deuteronomy 6:18 KJV)

And thou shalt love the Lord thy God with all thine heart, and with all thy soul, and with all thy might. (Deuteronomy 6:5 KJV)

Actually, the Choice Is Yours!

ᴄ◌◉◌৶

Finally, I'd like to make a confession to you. I have a real problem. The problem I have is that of being a father, a grandfather, and a great-grandfather. In other words, there are three generations involved. My children are all grown. My grandchildren are in double-digit numbers. Of course, my great-grandchildren, all three, are under five years of age. My personal problem, at least to me it feels like a problem or a responsibility, is that *I want all to go well for them. I want them all, all the time, to make good and very wise decisions I want them to be and stay on the right road in life all the time.*

My problem is to realize and accept the fact that I have no power, no ability, to decide for them. It's all, completely, entirely 100 percent left up to each of them to decide the course of their life.

Good or bad. Right or wrong. Also, I can't determine the consequences of their decisions. *It is out of my hands. The decisions and the consequences.*

The truth of the matter is, *that is life!* We each have the *awesome freedom and responsibility to choose our own way.* It's given to us and left up to us. Individually! *Free to be wise or free to be unwise.*

Joshua said to Israel:

> Choose you this day whom you will serve…
> but as for me and my house, we will serve the
> Lord." (Joshua 24:15 KJV)

God blesses those people who refuse evil advice and won't follow sinners or join in sneering at God. Instead, they find happiness in the teaching of the Lord, and they think about it day and night. Those people succeed in everything they do.

> That isn't true of those who are evil, they are like straw blown by the wind...and they won't have a place with the people of God." (Psalm 1:1, 4–5 CEV)

Read Psalm 1 again and Proverbs! Think about it!

Home Sickness Then and Now

⌘

There I was, nine years old, praying, kneeling beside my bed at my grandparent's house, near Rhine, Georgia. This was the same town where I was born—in a house, not a hospital.

I was praying for my parents to come and get me! I was very homesick.

That scene and that prayer happened almost every night for the entire three months of summer (June, July, and August) in 1944. That's where my younger brother, Larry, and I spent our summer vacations while out of school. At the end of the summer, we got a $1 bill and a pair of overalls for our pay!

During the days, we worked in the fields with my uncle and aunts. They were only a few years older than us. During the day, we were either working in the fields or caring for the mules, cows, and hogs. I never suffered from homesickness during the daytime. It was only when darkness came. The night was not good for me at nine years of age, and it was that way for all three months.

Now, years later, both Mom and Dad are gone. Dad left at eighty-six years old, and Mom died at ninety-six years old.

Some days now, I still greatly miss them. Reading the Bible, especially Psalm 3, Psalm 1, and Proverbs, reassures me that someday, I'll go HOME to see them—my heavenly home! I hope you, too, will find that reassurance and comfort!

Believe! Death Is Not the End!

‿௦௦ᦗ

Just recently, I've been reading a new book I bought. New in the sense that I just bought it and new in that the copyright is 2021. The title of the book is *AFTER*, written by a doctor, Bruce Greyson MD. In the book, he "explores what near-death experiences reveal about life and beyond." In essence, he declares from collaborative information from other scientists around the world, other countries, and from the information he gathered from nearly a thousand people who have "died" and "come back to life" that death is not the end of our existence.

Whether you call it the *mind* or the *soul*, our *existence*, our *consciousness, does not end at our death.*

He declares from a scientific viewpoint, after years of study and examination of personal testimonies of near-death experiences, that *death is not the end!*

You may want to read the book. And the Book! The Bible! Think about it. Jesus said the same thing over two thousand years ago!

> Jesus said, "I am the One who raises the dead to life! Everyone who has faith in me will live, even if they die." (John 11:25 CEV)

> And everyone who lives because of faith in Me will never really die. Do you believe this? (John 11:26 CEV)

> All who are wise follow a road that leads upward to life and away from death. (Proverbs 15:24 CEV)

About the Author

❧ ⟨☙⟩ ☙

After graduating from Norman College and Mercer University, Dr. Burnham earned his master of divinity degree from New Orleans Baptist Theological Seminary and received his doctorate from Eastern Baptist Theological Seminary in Philadelphia, Pennsylvania. He has earned his master of social work degree from the University of Georgia, completing his internship in the Department of Psychiatry and Health Behavior at the Medical College of Georgia. In addition, he received training in Clinical Pastoral Education at Spring Grove (Psychiatric) Hospital in Catonsville (Baltimore), Maryland. Other clinical training was received at the Wicomico Mental Health Center in Salisbury, Maryland. Further education includes studies at the Eastern Shore State (Psychiatric) Hospital in Maryland. He has attended continuing medical education seminars in Montreal, Vancouver, New York, New Orleans, Chicago, Atlanta, Orlando, Hilton Head, San Diego, and Hawaii.

He was a pastor for over thirty years, serving churches in Pennsylvania, Maryland, and Georgia.

Dr. Burnham was a licensed master of social work with over twenty-five years of experience as a psychotherapist.

He takes great pleasure in being the husband of Gayle, his wife, for over sixty years. They have four children: Linda, Dianne, Alan, and Wayne; eight grandchildren; and three great-grandchildren.

CPSIA information can be obtained
at www.ICGtesting.com
Printed in the USA
JSHW022125210323
39269JS00001B/3